AWAKENING ASTROLOGY

AWAKENING
ASTROLOGY

★

Five Key Planetary Energies for
PERSONAL TRANSFORMATION

★

MOLLY McCORD

Hierophantpublishing

Cover design by Laura Beers
Cover art by pixelparticle / Shutterstock.com
Arelix / Shutterstock.com
Print book interior design by Frame25 Productions

Hierophant Publishing
San Antonio, TX
www.hierophantpublishing.com

If you are unable to order this book from your local bookseller, you may order directly from the publisher.

Library of Congress Control Number: 2021952244
ISBN: 978-1-950253-23-4

10 9 8 7 6 5 4 3 2 1

*To Oliver, who continues to shine as
the sun, moon, and stars in my life.*

Contents

Introduction

Awakening Your Energetic Self

Imagine standing atop a tall stone tower in the Full Moon's glow, a passing wind gently caressing your cheek as you gaze up at the swirling motion of the stars in the night sky. The cool, brisk air continually opens up into a dark, endless abyss as you search for something—anything—that may catch your eye. Twinkling movements appear to come and go, and perhaps you see a glimpse of a shooting star. Off on the eastern horizon, you know the Sun will be returning to rise again, as it does every morning.

Yet there is much to take in during these still moments. Venus shines brightly on the darkest nights, but she appears in different places in the sky as the days and months pass by. The evening canvas is alive and evolving in a complex dance every day of the year. The mysteries of the Universe seem to be speaking to you through these heavenly bodies. But what does it all mean?

Ancient stargazers and scientists observed the night sky to find meaning, and to discover and understand how we relate to the solar system at large. Tall, massive structures called "star towers" were built to bring them closer to the heavens. As they watched and documented the changes in the sky, they perceived connections between human events and the patterns they saw there. In these first observatories, wise scholars interpreted the planetary movements as messages from the gods and deemed these movements significant in everyday life.

Western astrology has been documented as far back as 7,000 years, to the ancient Babylonian, Sumerian, and Egyptian civilizations. These cultures all boasted a rich tradition of keen star watchers who tracked the Sun and Moon, and the planets that were close to the Earth. Across hundreds of years, they began to make connections tying the agricultural cycles and harvests to the transiting Sun. In ancient Greece, doctors relied on birth charts to help determine their patients' ailments and subsequent remedies. When the planet Mars was prominent in the sky, it was often seen as a harbinger of coming war or some type of conflict. When an eclipse occurred and the sky went dark in the middle of the day, it was considered a message from the gods that great change was on the horizon. It was common for kings, queens, and privileged individuals to consult astrologers for guidance on political events, as well as for personal advice about when to hold weddings or significant occasions.

Astrology was first interpreted as a means of powerful communication between man and the heavens—an energetic dialogue that governed what was happening in the world. The messages received from the heavens were deemed either a blessing or a curse from the gods, and were taken very seriously. The Catholic celebration of Easter, for instance, has traditionally been connected with the lunar cycle, celebrated on the first Sunday after the first Full Moon following the spring equinox. Studying the stars has been considered highly relevant over long periods of time simply because it has proven to be accurate and insightful.

In our modern era, we now tap on our phones or screens to find instant answers to our deepest questions. We have advanced in our understanding of astrology beyond the general themes of the world at large and made connections to personal development and growth. Astrology has become more focused on individuals, especially thanks to the influence of Carl Jung, and has contributed to the growing connections we make today in areas of personal transformation. There's no need to build a stone tower in your neighborhood to find meaning in what the stars are communicating. Just turn to online sources or astrology apps or an ephemeris for guidance on what themes and energies are especially strong for you now.

As you dig into astrology a bit more, however, you may start to wonder how it actually works. How can planets in our solar system, which are thousands of miles away, have any personal effect on us? How can any of these energies really influence our personalities and our lives?

Astrology is a highly dynamic energy system that is connected to the cosmos—one that has continued to prove its relevance over centuries. In simple terms, astrology is a symbolic language that helps expand our personal consciousness and takes us beyond what our logical minds may grasp. Just as when we consult economic forecasts or turn to meteorologists for weather updates, astrology gives us a heads-up on what the energetic terrain will be in our lives and what to expect at specific times.

But in order to benefit from these messages, you must learn the language of astrology—the terminology, the glyphs, and the symbols that correspond to each of its particular energies. As you do so, you begin to discern what your own personal astrological chart reveals about your self-identity, your personal needs and desires, your life themes, and so much more. The nuances and particulars of this knowledge can sometimes seem overwhelming, however, now that so many sources of information are available to us. So it's only to be expected that you may arrive at a point where you wonder which parts of your astrological chart are the most essential to understand and apply. Or, if you're already familiar with some areas of astrology, you may be curious about the best path to follow to open up deeper interpretations and more intricate insights into your main energies.

Astrology can be approached from many different perspectives—Vedic (Sidereal), traditional (Hellenistic), mundane, evolutionary, medical, horary, electional, and more. Each of these perspectives acts like the lens or filter on a camera; as you change the lens, you shift what you see and how you interpret it. The astrological interpretation that I offer here is based on Western (Tropical) astrology. It focuses on the perspective of soul growth and higher-consciousness energies that you as a soul are working to fulfill in this lifetime. This may or may not resonate with you, and you may have your own preferred interpretations of this ancient art.

It is my intention here to offer you new ways to look at your astrological chart so you can gain a better understanding of yourself by awakening to a new understanding of your energies. I give simple, direct insights to guide you beyond basic astrological concepts and help you reach a new level of wisdom about yourself. I hope this information helps you connect with more of your true self and your unique energy in this lifetime. Your astrological chart holds many layers of energies, themes, and connections. As you go deeper into these expressions, you awaken to even more of yourself and the gifts that await you.

The Five Personal Planets

After decades of studying astrology and examining thousands of natal charts of clients around the globe, I have observed that the most profound self-revelations emerge from knowing more about your five personal planets: the Sun, the Moon, Mercury, Venus, and Mars. Every natal planet holds many meanings and themes related to your energy, but these five personal planets provide deeper insights into your inner workings and how your own personal energy system operates. Your natal Mercury sign, for instance, rules how you communicate and process information.

The five personal planets are connected to your core energies, which compose your self-identity, your personal needs, your mental processes, your wants and desires, and your ongoing areas of self-development. In fact, there are basic levels of astrological knowledge associated with each of these planets, and you may already be familiar with some of them. But if all of this is new to you, don't worry. We'll take a look at these basic meanings before we move on to more detailed discussions of each of your own personal planets.

Think of your five personal planets as your personal energetic recipe. Each one is a unique ingredient that contributes to your self-identity, as well as to how you experience your daily world. The opportunity to know yourself more intimately through these personal planets can enhance your self-understanding and your ability to live with purpose and meaning. In their simplest terms, you can think of these energies like this:

- *Your Sun sign* influences how you present yourself and shine your personality outward.

- *Your Moon sign* influences how you move through your daily life and respond to others.

- *Your Mercury sign* influences how you think, communicate, and digest information.

- *Your Venus sign* influences how you share and connect with others.

- *Your Mars sign* influences how you assert yourself and your needs.

Your Personal Energy Grid

At the exact minute and location when you were born, each planet was located in a particular area of the sky associated with a specific zodiac sign. The unique energies of these planets, combined with the energies of the sign they were in at your birth, exert an energetic influence on you throughout your life. Think of this as the energy that was "in the air" when you were born. We are energetic beings receiving and interacting with energies all the time, and every planet puts forth an energetic signature that you absorbed at the time of your birth. Astrology translates that energy into your life themes, your self-identity, and your personality traits. It is really amazing how accurate this system has proven to be over the centuries!

Let's take a brief look at the energies of each of your personal planets before we go deeper into their meanings. Then we'll look more closely at how all these energies interact in your astrological chart.

Solar Energies and Your Soul Growth Points

Your Sun sign is your main energetic essence in this lifetime. It guides your self-identity and your personality development. Many people focus on their Sun sign when they first discover astrology, as they soak in the information that is readily available about each of the twelve astrological Sun signs and what they mean. Yet as you advance in your self-awareness and astrological knowledge, you'll find that exploring your Sun sign can continue to reveal new insights.

Through my decades of astrological exploration, I have discovered how your Sun sign specifically can be further explored through four soul growth points. Astrology describes an energy system, and within this system your Sun sign is interconnected with other signs on the zodiac wheel. These four soul growth points comprise your Sun sign itself, your blind spot energies, your ongoing development, and your balancing energies. It is vital to understand your Sun sign's main intentions and expressions, but it is also fascinating to examine the overlays and deeper connections between these growth points so that you can work with them in a conscious way.

Your Sun energies are those of the sign the Sun was in at the time of your birth. Determining where this sign lies on the zodiac wheel provides you with a starting point for determining how the energies of your other personal planets will interact and guide you on your life journey. This is the sign you are most likely already most familiar with; this is what most people are referring to when they say, for example, "I am a Sagittarius."

Your blind spot energies then are those of the astrological sign that precedes your Sun sign on the zodiac wheel, moving around the wheel countercockwise. Knowing these energies redirects you to what you may overlook or forget at times. These are parts of yourself that you do not always see or willingly connect with as you go about your day. Yet working with these energies can help you reach out to new solutions, unseen possibilities, and different options that can be valuable, especially when you feel stuck, uncertain, or discouraged.

Your ongoing development energies are those of the astrological sign that follows your natal Sun sign on the zodiac wheel—again, moving counterclockwise around the wheel. These remind you that you are always growing and evolving. You can embrace these developmental stages and open up to them when you want to move forward or set new intentions for your life direction. Your ongoing development reveals where you have more to learn and understand and where you are capable of opening up to new life themes and intentions.

Your balancing energies, which are those of the sign opposite your Sun sign on the astrological wheel, are associated with attributes you can turn to for grounding, perspective, and detachment. These energies can help you depersonalize and step back from situations so you can see other viewpoints. You can incorporate wisdom from the strengths of your balancing sign to help you uncover new solutions and a higher understanding of yourself and others. Incorporating your balancing sign energies connects you with the vast array of ways to learn, grow, and integrate more of who you are in your daily life.

Everything is connected. The Sun's vitality is interconnected with all astrological signs. When you incorporate these additional insights into your understanding, you discover more ways to work with your soul growth in a supportive and holistic manner.

Lunar Energies

Your birth time is very important, both astrologically and energetically, because it reveals when you took your first breath as a sovereign being in the world—when you left your mother's energy behind and became a discrete individual. Astrologers use the time of your birth to ascertain your Moon sign, which is connected with your emotional self, your inner needs, what feels good to you, and how your energy is designed to navigate your daily world.

Just as you can connect with more energies through your Sun sign, you can also go deeper into the hidden realms of your Moon sign's energy imprint. You may discover that you've been carrying and holding energies your whole life based on what was happening at the time of your birth, both in terms of the heavens and in terms of your relationship to your mother in that moment. Your Moon sign reveals your emotional world, and how and why you feel, receive, react, and interpret experiences in the way you do. It reflects your first unconscious experiences with your mother or mother figure and how her energy imprinted what you felt about being loved, seen, and acknowledged as you became your own separate being in the world. This can help you understand how you may have responded to people based on primal energetic experiences with your mother.

Mercury Energies

Your natal Mercury sign indicates how you think, how you receive information, how you make decisions, and how you communicate. Your Mercurial expression is thus key to understanding how you perceive the world around you, as well as knowing what your mind needs in order to process and contemplate your life choices. Our modern lives offer more mental stimulus than we humans have ever had at any other time in our evolutionary past. Many struggle with an excess of mental energy, always seeking answers, solutions, and knowledge, and relentlessly gnawing away at themselves to the point of anxiety, worry, and mental stress. Mercury can provide a powerful key to rebalancing these mental energies.

By understanding the astrological sign opposite your natal Mercury sign, you can come into greater harmony. The first step is to understand your habitual internal workings, the ways that your Mercury sign naturally communicates and thinks. Then you can step out of these behaviors by calling on the energies of the opposing sign. Opening to another perspective can help you find relief from mental pressure and tension. This opposing sign can offer you a fresh viewpoint so you don't stay locked in your head. The more you understand this balancing sign, the more tools you have to work with and integrate into your life as needed.

Venus Energies

Your natal Venus sign reveals how you relate to others based on what you enjoy, how you prefer to share, what you need to feel loved, and how you interact from a place of self-acceptance. Venus relates to your self-worth and self-love energies that allow you to continue to elevate and grow through higher consciousness. This personal planet also reveals your ability to be receptive. It determines how you feel about receiving and what your heart needs to feel seen and loved. Your Venus energies help you love yourself and be more confident in your own energy field.

Your natal Venus also pertains to your relationships with others. In fact, your loved ones may have a better sense of your Venus attributes than you do, since these are the qualities in you that others see and get to know and love.

Venus is deeply connected with feminine energies. This planet determines how you receive and feel love from others, as well as how you express archetypal feminine qualities of receiving, creating, and nurturing. Working with your natal Venus can help you to know your own feminine energies better and learn how to raise your vibration in their expression.

Mars Energies

Mars energy is associated with your physical body, your daily energy levels, what motivates you, and how you go after what you want. Mars can be the healthy ego and confidence you exude in the world. This natal planet also connects to how you express masculine energies, as well as the male energies you are drawn to and exhibit in yourself.

Have you ever wondered why your motivation may be inconsistent or why you may hesitate to act at times? Do you ever want to go after something and then observe how your method of doing so varies from that of your friends or family? Your natal Mars reveals more about your ability to assert yourself, and you can call on its strengths through the conscious expression of masculine energies. Direct your physical body, your healthy ego, and your intentional desires toward what you truly want, and your Mars will be invigorated to go after more of what matters to you. Your Mars energies can be courageously expressed through growing confidence, greater clarity, and taking action in appropriate ways. They shine a guiding light for you to create, build, and manifest the life you want to lead.

Your Astrological Chart

In order to understand the role these five personal planets play in your astrological chart, you must consider six key components: signs, planets, houses, aspects, elements, and modalities. Let's look briefly at each of these.

The Twelve Signs

For those brand-new to the fascinating system of astrology, the night sky is divided into twelve sections, or *signs*, that we refer to together as the zodiac wheel. Natal astrological charts are laid out on this wheel. These twelve signs reveal a progression of energy, beginning with Aries and ending with Pisces, moving counterclockwise around the wheel. Each of the astrological signs embodies certain themes, needs, and intentions that include a spectrum of energies from lower expressions to higher expressions. In the figure below, these signs are displayed in a circle, with twelve distinct areas that are called "houses" (see below).

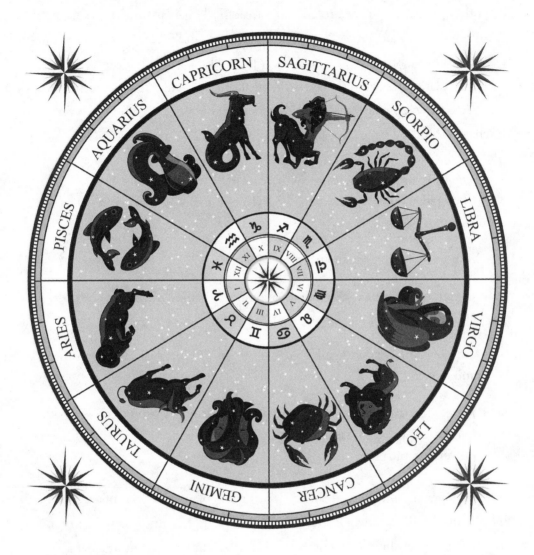

The Ten Planets

Our solar system is composed of luminaries and planets that have astrological significance because each one pertains to different archetypes and themes. In this book, we will examine the Sun, the Moon, Mercury, Venus, and Mars to learn how they can be used as tools for personal understanding and transformation. The other planets that play a role in an astrological chart include Jupiter, Saturn, Uranus, Neptune, and Pluto. Asteroids like Chiron and Ceres are also becoming more relevant in astrology, as is the dwarf planet Eris.

Every planet has multiple layers of meaning. We will explore the meanings of the five personal planets in the chapters that follow. Here is a brief overview of what each of the other five planets represents:

- *Jupiter* is associated with growth, learning, expansion, higher knowledge, support, and beneficial developments and outcomes.

- *Saturn* relates to applied effort, hard work, commitments, dedication, responsibility, and maturity.

- *Uranus* reveals unexpected developments, rebellion, future potentials, collective themes, and awakening energies.

- *Neptune* connects with spiritual growth, intuition, idealism, escapism, and trusting what is unknown.

- *Pluto* encourages deep transformation, evolutionary growth, permanent life changes, and restructuring life with a new sense of power and purpose.

Astrologers have observed the cycles of these planets for centuries. Through this accumulated knowledge, we have gained a higher understanding of how planetary energies show up in our lives and what they represent in a natal astrological chart. After considering these planetary energies in a natal chart, we then look at the placement of the planets in the twelve different houses.

The Twelve Houses

The zodiac wheel is divided into twelve individual segments called "houses." Each of these houses represents distinct areas of life or specific environments, beginning with the sign rising above the eastern horizon at the time of your birth, called your Ascendant. This energy is associated with your physical appearance, the first impression you make, and how you present yourself to others. It is also the beginning point of your *1st house*, which rules your self-identity, your body, your personal needs, and how you know yourself. The remaining houses chart a progression of self-understanding moving counterclockwise around the zodiac wheel.

- *The 2nd house* rules your personal value system, your self-worth, and your financial priorities.

- *The 3rd house* determines your communication, your learning style, your daily priorities, and your relationship with siblings.

- *The 4th house* relates to personal space, emotional expression, and what makes you feel at home.

- *The 5th house* connects with creative style, risk-taking, courage, and developing personal confidence.

- *The 6th house* reveals your physical health, your daily responsibilities, your work, and how you enjoy being of service to others.

- *The 7th house* represents partnerships, cooperation, and how you interact with others in all areas of your life.

- *The 8th house* shows how you share your needs, your resources, and your true feelings with others.

- *The 9th house* highlights your beliefs and life philosophy, travel, and higher education.

- *The 10th house* influences your career, your professional expression, your public status, and how you are recognized by others.

- *The 11th house* inspires your life directions, your ability to give back, how you work in collective projects, and the people you know casually, like friends and acquaintances.

- *The 12th house* focuses on completions, forgiveness, spiritual growth, and taking a break from the real world.

There is much more to each of these twelve houses, but this gives with a general overview of their meaning and influence.

The Four Major Aspects

Aspects are the "conversations," the connection points, that occur between planets. These aspects are determined by the number of degrees separating two or more planets on the zodiac wheel. Aspects essentially tell us how the planets are getting along—or not. Are they in agreement and supporting each other? Or are they projecting discord and lack of connection?

Two planets that are on opposite sides of the zodiac wheel (180° apart) are in an aspect called "opposition," which can signal tension, struggle, or the need to find a balance point between competing energies. Planets that are close together in the same zodiac sign are said to be in "conjunction," which means they are on the same page, so to speak, and share the same intentions. Other major aspects include a "trine," which occurs when planets are 120° apart, and a "square," which indicates a distance of 90° between two or more planets. A deeper look at aspects is outside the scope of this book, but it is important to understand what they are generally in your natal chart as you delve more deeply into your energies.

The Four Elements

You are composed of many types of energies, and one way to examine them in your chart is through the filter of the four elements: Earth, Air, Water, and Fire. Each of the twelve astrological signs is associated with one of these elements.

Look around at the beauty of our world, and you'll see how each of these elements is alive and thriving in its own unique way. Simply visualizing each of these elements helps us to understand their attributes and themes, which also helps further define our needs and priorities in an individual way. In addition, you can physically connect with the elements in your chart to make them come alive, to call on their wisdom, or to invite them to bring balance and peace. Soaking in warm water, breathing fresh air, putting your hands in the soil, or warming yourself by a crackling fire—these are all ways to recenter your elemental energies.

- *Earth energies* are associated with patience, diligence, strength, focus, responsibility, boundaries, financial awareness, and practicality.

- *Air energies* are connected with communication techniques, socializing, cooperation, ideas, projects, relationships, mental processes, and objectivity.

- *Water energies* embody emotions, connection, sharing, intimacy, trust, intuition, subjectivity, and compassion.

- *Fire energies* are related to motivation, inspiration, action, impulsiveness, the ego, competitiveness, and enthusiasm.

There are three astrological signs connected with each of the four elements. Earth is identified with Taurus, Virgo, and Capricorn. Air is identified with Gemini, Libra, and Aquarius. Water is identified with Cancer, Scorpio, and Pisces. Fire is identified with Aries, Leo, and Sagittarius. The importance of these identifications will become clearer as you read through the following chapters.

The Three Modalities

The turning of the zodiac wheel corresponds to the progression of time throughout the year. This progression can be further understood through the three modalities that relate to this passage of time: the cardinal, the fixed, and the mutable. Each season—spring, summer, fall, and winter—starts with a cardinal sign, then moves to a fixed sign, and then into a mutable sign. In the Northern Hemisphere, Aries begins spring, Cancer begins summer, Libra begins fall, and Capricorn begins winter. In this way, the flow of energy through the seasons unfolds in tandem with the turning of the zodiac wheel.

Each cardinal sign begins a new season. The fixed signs then stabilize each season, reflecting the necessary qualities that need to grow and develop during that time of the year. For example, the seeds planted during the beginning of spring in Aries begin to take root and grow stronger under the influence of Taurus energies.

Finally, mutable signs offer possibilities, choices, and adaptability as one season comes to an end and preparation for the next season begins. The firm roots of Taurus nourish many buds that grow and diversify during the mutable experience of Gemini, preparing the flowers to bloom fully as summer begins with Cancer.

Each of these three modalities is connected to four astrological signs:

♦ *The cardinal signs* are Aries, Cancer, Libra, and Capricorn.

♦ *The fixed signs* are Taurus, Leo, Scorpio, and Aquarius.

♦ *The mutable signs* are Gemini, Virgo, Sagittarius, and Pisces.

Knowing the modalities of your five personal planet signs will help you understand how you are likely to move through life, including how you approach change and new directions, as well as how you prefer to operate in your daily routines and habits.

Masculine and Feminine Energies

Another layer of meaning for astrology is found in masculine and feminine energies. Regardless of your gender or sex, you possess both these energy signatures, which provide further insights into how you navigate through your life, how you perceive yourself, and what matters to you.

Masculine energy is associated with your Sun sign, and with the Fire and Air signs. Some general masculine qualities include action, intention, stability, mental processes, self-assertion, protection, providing, independence, ego, and strength. These qualities are associated with father energy, although this does not necessarily indicate a biological father. It can be anyone who acted as a father figure to you. Father energy is connected with your first experiences of security, boundaries, responsibility, and strength—qualities that developed as your sense of self was being shaped and you were encouraged to become an individual who could stand on your own two feet. Father energy provides structure to who you are and how you approach the world at large.

Divine Masculine energies are expressed through the more evolved masculine qualities that emerge through conscious growth. As you do healing work and shadow work around your masculine qualities, you become more awakened to the higher expressions of these parts of yourself. These are your Divine Masculine energies.

For example, when you reflect on your career, you may realize that your ego exerted itself strongly in a particular job in order to demonstrate your power and control. You may have come across in a way that pushed people away or created tension with others. As you awaken to this behavior in yourself, however, you realize that you can still feel powerful and in control while also generating trust and respect from others. When you awaken to this, you no longer want to come across as threatening or domineering; you have evolved your leadership style to be more aware of how others perceive you.

Essentially, Divine Masculine energy develops when you have healed parts of your unconscious masculine energies and now hold yourself to a more evolved, conscious expression of those traits. This energy combines the strength of the mind and body with the higher awareness of the heart.

Feminine energy is associated with your Moon sign and with the Earth and Water signs. General feminine qualities include nurturing, creativity, trust, receptivity, emotion, safety, flow, openness, heart, and connection. They are most closely connected with the energy of your mother or a mother figure. Again, this does not have to be a biological mother. Rather it relates to your first unconscious experiences of receiving love, connecting at a primal level, learning to trust, and feeling nurtured and safe. Think of this in terms of how you received love at a young age and whether your needs were met on a consistent basis.

Divine Feminine energies are the more conscious expressions of feminine qualities that support the continual opening and flow of loving energies that create a connection with others. These qualities are parts of yourself that have been acknowledged, healed, and loved, which expands your ability to offer this energy to others.

For example, many unhealed feminine qualities can be experienced and felt through relationships with other people. Perhaps you had a sibling, a friend, or a partner in your life who hurt you deeply at some point, and this was a catalyst for growth in your healing work. This relationship may have triggered you to look at something unconscious within yourself—like ways in which you were not trusting yourself—and given you a new perspective on why you were not listening to your needs or feelings. As you come into greater awareness of your lack of self-trust, you gain the ability to be more attentive to your internal messages and to acknowledge them. You commit to honoring yourself more. This new consciousness opens up a deeper connection to yourself, your heart, and your needs, which you can then confidently share with others because you have healed that part of yourself.

Your Divine Feminine essence reminds you to be loving, kind, and compassionate to yourself and to connect with others through that expression. This energy combines the power of your emotions and intuition with the strength of your individuality.

Divine Masculine qualities can also be viewed as how you exert your energy *in* the world, while Divine Feminine qualities are how you receive energy *from* the world. The chapters that follow will help you to see these aspects of yourself in a new way, especially as these qualities relate to your personal planets and how you interact in relationships.

How to Use This Book

Each section of this book is devoted to one of the five personal planets. Each begins with a short chapter that illuminates more about what the planet means generally and some of the ways it may operate in your life. I suggest reading each of these chapters before you move on to the chapters that give specific information about your own personal Sun, Moon, Mercury, Venus, or Mars sign. I also invite you to read the entries for other signs that may hold meaning when considered in relationship to your personal planetary signs. This is especially true for the three additional signs that comprise your soul growth points in your Sun sign.

I also encourage you to delve into the signs of other people in your life. Knowing the Moon signs of your mother and your children, for example, can be enlightening. Beyond that, looking up the signs and attributes of the personal planets of people you know, or even people with whom you find yourself in conflict or opposition, can inform your best course of action and pave the way for mutually beneficial relationships and interactions.

For most of us, astrology can be an enriching tool for personal growth that is easily and fruitfully combined with our other emotional, educational, and spiritual practices and beliefs. I share a few of my own beliefs here as they relate to soul evolution and growth over many lifetimes, for example. I invite you to incorporate everything that is meaningful to you on your own astrological journey, and to place anything that doesn't resonate for you off to the side. Astrology takes us on a self-directed journey of self-discovery. We all have our feet planted on the same Earth, and we all look up in wide-eyed wonder at the same stars and planets swirling around us. But we are all beautiful, singular expressions of our own personal energies. This is *your* journey.

Astrology can be simple and straightforward, but it can also be complex. This book offers an entry point into what I believe are the most potent energies in your natal chart—the ones that are especially fruitful to explore if you are new to astrology. Of course, there are even more layers to explore if you choose to do so. In the pages that follow, I sometimes refer to astrological concepts and terms that fall beyond the scope of this book. I encourage you to dive more deeply into the vast world of astrological wisdom if you feel called to do so.

As you will discover, astrology is a rich and deep art. For some, it brings up memories and insights they may want to return to at a later time for self-reflection, meditation, or further personal understanding. It may thus be beneficial to keep a small journal handy as you read through these chapters. Write down basic information on the relationships between your planets and signs to use for reference later. Record any flashes of personal insight that may come to you. These notes can become an invaluable part of your astrological explorations.

Understanding your five personal planets will help you gain new insights into your life patterns and themes and potentially clarify what you really want to create in your life and how to do it. Astrology is a powerful tool for expanding your self-awareness and opening up to the infinite potential in the Universe. I hope this book provides revelations about the choices, decisions, and actions you have always gravitated toward in your life, as well as why your personal growth is a powerful force in this lifetime. As you awaken to more of your energetic imprint through astrology, you may notice self-verifying patterns in your life and in your energy. There are areas of your life that only you can know and understand based on your own experiences.

Awakening Astrology will connect you to deeper layers of the energy field you experience and use every day. Your Sun's guiding light is always shining, just as your Moon is always bathing you in its gentle glow. Your Mercury is actively thinking and interacting with the world, while your Venus and Mars energies are each demonstrating what you want, value, and need. These are the energies that you work with every day. Getting to know each one more fully can connect you to the profound guidance and potential that lies within you.

PART ONE

Your Sun Sign

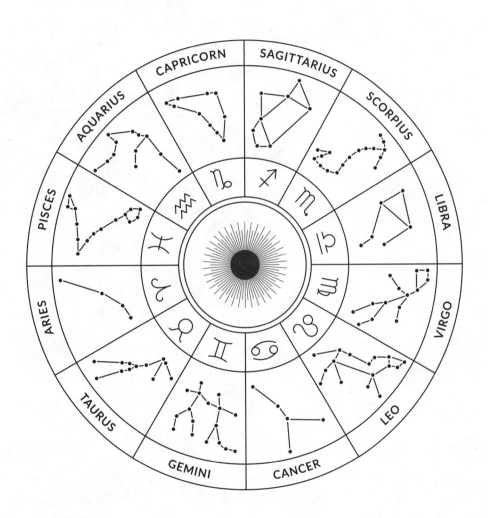

Chapter 1

Solar Energies

Most people enter the world of astrology through their Sun sign, especially since that is the most commonly referenced horoscope information in magazines, newspapers, and online videos. Perhaps this is how your interest in astrology was first piqued. You may have learned at an early age that your Sun was in Virgo or Aquarius, and then used this knowledge to search for more about your personality. At some point, you may even have wondered how more than seven billion people on this planet could be divided up into only twelve different Sun signs, or how people with the same Sun sign could be so different from each other. Sun-sign astrology is fascinating. But it is also limiting, since it only gives a part of the picture.

Your Sun sign gives you good bite-size, general information about yourself, but as you learn more about your astrological energies, your whole natal chart comes alive. When your understanding of your Sun sign flourishes and grows in cooperation with these other energies, you gain a clearer understanding of the entirety of your unique astrological chart. Where you may once have thought of yourself as a Sagittarius or a Cancer, you come to understand that your particular Sun sign contains a multitude of other energetic aspects within it. This is how we can be so similar to our fellow Sun-sign mates, and yet so different.

Western Tropical astrology is associated with the four seasons of the calendar year, which are fixed dates on the calendar. It assigns astrological signs to these periods of time based on these calendar dates. Below is a summary of the dates of each astrological sign, but please note that these can shift to a day before or a day after these specific dates each year, depending on whether it is a Leap Year and where you are on the globe.

- *Aries*: March 21–April 19

- *Taurus*: April 20–May 20

- *Gemini*: May 21–June 20

- *Cancer*: June 21–July 22

- *Leo*: July 23–August 22

- *Virgo*: August 23–September 22

- *Libra*: September 23–October 22

- *Scorpio*: October 23–November 21

- *Sagittarius*: November 22–December 21

- *Capricorn*: December 22–January 20

- *Aquarius*: January 21–February 18

- *Pisces*: February 19–March 20

One of the best ways to deepen your understanding of your Sun sign is to look at its neighbors on the zodiac wheel. As we discussed in the introduction, for each Sun sign there are three additional signs that provide key insights and opportunities. Along with your Sun sign itself, these make up what I call your four points of soul growth:

- *Your Sun sign* shines as your brightest light.

- *Your energetic blind spot* embodies qualities that are more difficult for you to access.

- *Your ongoing development* sign provides opportunities for personal growth and transformation.

- *Your balancing energy* brings the attributes of your dynamic opposite to your life path.

Exploring these four points of growth in relationship brings you into a deeper knowledge of what your Sun sign means for you.

Four Points of Soul Growth

In my view, each soul physically incarnates in the energy of a specific Sun sign by choice. You arrived at your earthly existence—at a specific time and in a specific place—on purpose. Whether you believe this or not—either literally or in a metaphorical sense—I invite you to explore this idea and see what it helps you uncover in your psyche. It may bring a deep sense of meaning to your life.

Sun Sign Energy

Your Sun sign is your first point of soul growth. It guides you as you develop confidence and strength and a higher consciousness in yourself. The Sun is the biggest light in our solar system; it blazes with life-giving energy. Your Sun sign thus reveals how and where you will shine, flourish, and grow. The energies of your Sun sign invite you to understand more about your needs, your gifts, and your self-identity, and provide guidance on how you will mature energetically throughout your lifetime.

Blind Spot Energy

Your second point of soul growth is your energetic blind spot. This is the astrological sign that comes *before* your natal Sun sign on the zodiac wheel (moving counterclockwise). Just like a blind spot you may experience while driving a car, this area requires that you make an extra effort to see clearly. It requires greater consciousness to access. These energetic blind spots can hide areas of discomfort or challenge for you. For example, if you were born with the Sun in Leo, you may not naturally tap into the energies of Cancer, the previous sign. This can create a potential energetic blind spot for you in the areas that Cancer rules, including vulnerability and inner authenticity. Every sign in the zodiac holds its own gifts and intentions. And, just as double-checking your car's blind spots increases your safety and ease on the road, tuning in to these energetic blind spots can provide important support for your Sun sign's natural tendencies.

Your potential blind spot energy will always be connected with a different element (Earth, Air, Water, Fire), a different modality (cardinal, fixed, mutable), and a different expression (masculine or feminine) than your Sun sign. This sounds complicated, but all it means is that your blind spot invites and challenges you to explore a wider range of experiences. What are you overlooking or ignoring? Depending on your personal chart, these blind spots may be more or less accessible to you, especially if you have other planets that already fall in this particular sign, especially the Moon, Mercury, Venus, or Mars. If your natal Sun is in Leo, for instance, but you have Mercury or Venus in Cancer, the traits of vulnerability and authenticity may already feel familiar to you.

Ongoing Development Energy

Your third point of soul growth is your ongoing development. This is the astrological sign that appears *after* your Sun sign on the zodiac wheel (again, moving counterclockwise). It reveals how you can further mature your self-identity and personality traits in this lifetime. For example, if your natal Sun is in Sagittarius, then your ongoing development occurs through the qualities of Capricorn: organizing, managing, and providing structure. Understanding this sign can show you how to explore more of your own energy potentials. This energy can feel uncomfortable or foreign, since it is always a different element, modality, and expression than your natal Sun sign. You may feel it more naturally if you already have planets in your ongoing development sign, especially the Moon, Mercury, Venus, or Mars.

Balancing Energy

The fourth point of soul growth is your balancing energy. This is the astrological sign that lies *opposite* your Sun sign on the zodiac wheel. Your balancing energy is your dynamic opposite. We understand things as much by what they are not as by what they are. This sign provides perspective on your Sun sign through its opposing energies and intentions. You can tune in to your balancing energy in order to detach and step away from your ego, your self-identity, and your subjectivity in a way that gives you a bigger perspective. Think of a seesaw. You always know where you are in relationship to the opposite end of the board—whether up, down, or in a perfect state of balance. The qualities of the sign that opposes your Sun sign can offer this same perspective. For example, if your Sun is in Virgo, Pisces energies may help you step away from the need to figure everything out or the tendency to be in your head too much.

Your balancing energy is always in the same expression (masculine or feminine) and the same modality (cardinal, fixed, mutable) as your Sun sign. But it is in a complementary element that works synergistically with your Sun sign (Air and Fire signs, or Water and Earth signs). This energy thus keeps you from being too much in your self-identity and helps you remember that you are connected to a vast field of energies and potentials that you can choose to tap into on a regular basis.

The four soul growth point energies thus encapsulate every element, all three modalities, and both expressions, giving you a special combination of energies that balance you and allow you to integrate the full spectrum of astro-logical energies into your consciousness and your energy field.

Chapter 2

The Twelve Sun Signs

In this chapter, we'll look at each of the twelve Sun signs on the zodiac wheel. Here you will find each sign's unique opportunities and the challenges it presents on the soul's journey toward growth in this lifetime. For each sign, I also give brief notes on its corresponding blind spot, ongoing development, and balancing energies, as well as an explanation of the sign's potential for personal growth.

The Sun in Aries (Fire, Cardinal, Masculine)

Pioneer, Leader, Child, Warrior, Maverick, Lone Wolf

The soul's intention to incarnate through the Sun sign of Aries signals a desire to initiate new experiences and energies in this lifetime. Aries energy expresses its gifts of courage, instigation, and independence, thus those with the Sun in Aries feel a driving need to live life on their own terms and to develop their independence. They will be challenged at times to be the first to do something and may find themselves stepping away from a crowd or group. They may receive an idea or inspiration or want to take action before others do. They may be drawn to doing new things that both scare them and invigorate them.

Aries is the first Fire sign on the zodiac wheel. It initiates spring as the first cardinal sign in the calendar. Like all Fire signs, Aries emits and embraces masculine energy. As an Aries, you are equipped with the courage to go first, but you must also pay attention to the details and the next steps. Take the time to ascertain what is worth your energetic commitment; otherwise you could find yourself starting many things and finishing none of them. You can burn hot and quick, moving on to new pursuits as others toil away toward success. But this can sometimes leave you feeling adrift, without enough sustained commitments to ground you.

With your Sun in Aries, you are energetically designed to be a leader and to create your place in the world, in whatever ways you feel called to trust yourself and your ideas. Your Aries energy works to know itself continually and through ongoing self-discovery. By understanding who you are at a soul level, you return to the source of your courage and drive.

Harnessing Aries energy involves knowing when to slow down and think things through before acting. Before responding, overcommitting, or even deciding what to do, practice taking a few moments to imagine the entire path to your desired outcome in a methodical way. Be mindful of your daily energy and conscious of your body's needs and wants. Because you have so much energy to burn, you probably require regular exercise and physical movement. This will allow the energy to flow through your body without getting backed up or blocked. Trust this in yourself. Even if you find yourself trying a variety of exercises and only doing them for a short period of time, keep moving and follow what your body is calling you to do.

Invest in leadership development to support your ability to assert yourself in healthy ways and lead others in a broader capacity. Stay aware of how you come across to others. Ask for and process feedback that can help you develop your talents with people. Intentionally listen to various ideas, opinions, and information that can support how you communicate and interact with others. This can help ward off your tendency to retreat into your own private bubble.

As an Aries, you are an initiator. You are gifted with beginning tasks, projects, ideas, and anything that inspires you, yet you may notice that you need the support of others to carry through on long-term tasks, work, and details. Depending on your personal astrological chart, you may be best suited for getting things started, but not be the right person to do the regular maintenance or ongoing work. Knowing this about yourself can help set you up for success. Aries energy can be very fast-moving—sometimes too fast for a group environment—so stay mindful of how you lead and/or interact with others.

Soul Growth in Aries

Souls with the Sun in Aries are here to learn and grow, and to do things for the first time. If this is your natal Sun, you may find yourself on the leading edge in your life. When not in a leadership capacity, you may not want to take directions or be told what to do, as you can be quite headstrong in how you want to proceed. Be mindful of where your place is in an organization, hierarchy, or group environment. You may even notice a theme of branching out and doing your own thing because you feel as if you can be yourself when you trust your own style and need to assert yourself.

Your physical self and body awaken through messages from the Aries-ruled areas of the head, eyes, skin, brain, and blood flow. You may feel a flush of heat in your skin or a surge of energy in your body that reminds you to calm any excessive expressions of anger, overreaction, frustration, or impatience.

In fact, many individuals with the Sun in Aries need to develop strategies for dealing with anger and impatience throughout their lives. You may need to focus on breathing, meditation, calming routines, bodywork, or other intentional practices that support moving the rush of energy through your system in a healthy way. Stay aware of what triggers your impulsive reactions or anger, as you may notice themes. Calming down your reactions allows you to invest in your long-term growth and well-being and to manage your formidable energy on a daily basis.

As you mature, you may look back and find you have been unconsciously childish or selfish in your needs, as well as in your expectations of others. If you don't get your own way, how do you handle these situations? Do you have expectations that others should always tend to your needs or place you first? By looking back on these unconscious patterns with compassion and curiosity, you can decide to change your behavior in the future.

As an Aries, you have decided at a soul level that this lifetime will require you to awaken to what it means to be independent and stand up for yourself. You are ready for new experiences and fresh ways to assert yourself that can be both exhilarating and nerve-racking. You enjoy the chase and the next adventure, so follow what calls to you. Being an individual is crucial for you.

Blind Spot Energy: Pisces (Water, Mutable, Feminine)

As the sign that precedes Aries on the zodiac wheel, Pisces energy reminds you to detach from what you want, step back from the ego, and remember that surrender can be an effective strategy for driving something forward. Aries energy can be impatient, but Pisces taps into the flow of life that does not require force or speed. Furthermore, if you can release your tendency to become overly invested in one particular outcome, you will feel a deeper trust in life, knowing you can rely on the Universe to support you behind the scenes of your desires. Think of the flow of vast networks of underground water. Pisces will support your ability to trust in a calm approach at times, reminding you that you are more than what appears on the surface.

Read the section on the Sun in Pisces for more information on the attributes and qualities you may want to keep in your awareness to support your Aries journey.

Ongoing Development: Taurus (Earth, Fixed, Feminine)

The initiative and creativity of Aries energy benefit from the ongoing development energy of Taurus, the sign that follows Aries on the zodiac wheel. In learning from Taurus, Aries takes concrete form and shape and works through steady, practical next steps. Practice slowing down and being intentional with your expectations. Stay mindful of where you are directing your energy and look for how your efforts can be implemented with a practical payoff. Understand that most things take time to build and grow. You may have a million ideas or adventures you want to pursue, and calling on fixed-sign Taurus' intentions will support purposeful decision-making to narrow down the field. It can also allow for the time and stamina it takes to see something through to completion.

Read the section on the Sun in Taurus for more information on the attributes and qualities you may want to keep in your awareness.

Balancing Energy: Libra (Air, Cardinal, Masculine)

Libra energies oppose those of Aries on the zodiac wheel. They provide an objective, broader perspective that can help individuals with the Sun in Aries step away from their individualistic sphere to see how others may experience or perceive things. Libra energy can help with talking things through, examining different angles of an interaction, and understanding more about people and their behavior. The balancing energies of Libra remind Aries that you do not have to go it alone all of the time. Relationships are a necessary and beneficial part of your journey.

Read the section on the Sun in Libra for more information on the attributes and qualities you may want to keep in your awareness.

Sun in Taurus (Earth, Fixed, Feminine)

Builder, Musician, Peacekeeper, Investor, Naturalist

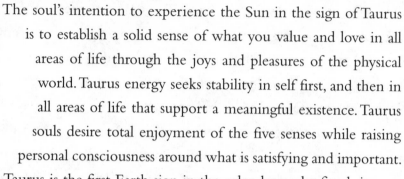

The soul's intention to experience the Sun in the sign of Taurus is to establish a solid sense of what you value and love in all areas of life through the joys and pleasures of the physical world. Taurus energy seeks stability in self first, and then in all areas of life that support a meaningful existence. Taurus souls desire total enjoyment of the five senses while raising personal consciousness around what is satisfying and important.

Taurus is the first Earth sign in the calendar, and a fixed sign on the zodiac wheel. It has a feminine energy. This combination yields groundedness, perseverance, and deep connection. Taurus individuals are tasked with grounding their sense of self in the world without overidentifying with material gain, status, possessions, or what can be accumulated. They experience a driving need for stability amid the storms and chaos of life. Early on in their journey, they may try to grab hold of security through financial gain and building a lifestyle that protects against uncertainty and change. But as Taurus souls mature through life experiences, they can realize the potential of the securest place of all—within themselves. They can find the stability and safety they crave in the internal foundations of self-worth and self-love. Taurus souls can develop internal energy centers that are untouchable to outside forces, leading them to a solid mountain of self-assured higher consciousness.

Taurus is typically associated with our most basic, primal needs for survival. How do you build a life for yourself that resonates with your values? Whether on a farm with acres of land or in a skyscraper condo, you want to live on your own terms and with a mindfulness of the costs of life. Money, finances, and economics are Taurus-ruled areas, and if this is your sign, you will be drawn to making a practical assessment of choices, including what to buy, how much to spend, and how to invest in ways that provide an acceptable return on investment over the years. However, it is important to look at what belief systems are driving money matters in your life. Are there habits, patterns, and perceptions that were ingrained in childhood or from your parents? You may realize you want to shift your values or change your perception around money matters, especially as you go out into the real world and build your own life for yourself. You may question the purpose of money and what it truly means to you, aside from paying bills and eating at your favorite restaurant. Your focus on money and finances can be connected to Taurus' driving need for stability, but what are the deeper questions underneath this fascination? Your notion of worth and value extends beyond material needs and into your sense of self.

Soul Growth in Taurus

Taurus souls seek to establish a higher sense of self-worth in this lifetime. They need to be appreciated and valued by others in a clear, loving way that is based on who they truly are and not on what they own, or buy, or have in the world. Though they crave worthiness in the eyes of others, their most important priority is to see it in themselves. With a Sun in Taurus, you may have to stand up for yourself or speak up about what you need in order for others to hear you fully. Your lifetime may include multiple opportunities to demonstrate self-reliance. You may be called to step away from what others expect of you, including the expectation that you should share everything or provide for the needs of others too much. Stay mindful of how much you receive in return, and seek out reciprocal, balanced relationships. While you may strongly identify with your possessions, your bank account, or your financial portfolio, when you tap into your own natural connection to abundance, you will feel stable and secure in your ability to manifest everything you need on a regular basis.

Asserting your worthiness to others may be a perennial theme in your lifetime. Do you think that you are worthy of a raise you have not received? Do you feel undervalued or not fully seen for your talents? Do you resent not being heard in a conversation? All of these can come from a solid sense of your own self-worth. As you understand what you need, you can be clearer in how you show up in your authentic energy. You are learning to love yourself and feel valuable in all areas of your life, including career, relationships, family matters, and friendships.

Taurus individuals crave harmony in their social environment. Your challenge here may be to honor what you need without shutting out trustworthy people and to sustain relationships through the ups and downs of life. You may experience significant life events that relate to trust—whom you can trust and with whom you can share core values. You may be tested to remain strong and rooted in yourself during times of uncertainty and change.

As you develop more trust in yourself, you feel steadiness and peace with the bigger cycles of life's changes. Taurus is an Earth sign that can exude a calming influence over yourself and others. When the going gets tough, the fixed intentions of Taurus can become tougher and stronger, staying the course for a desired outcome. You will see what you want through to completion. Call it perseverance or stubbornness, but know that this type of determination can be a powerful guiding force.

Staying mindful of what you need will pave the way for soul growth. While this is true for everyone to a certain degree, those with the Sun in Taurus take inspiration from a grounded physical environment that energetically speaks to them. Typically, the Earth signs need to feel in communion with the natural elements. Time alone in nature, growing a garden, walking in a forest, and listening to the birds all nourish and replenish you. The soul's desire to experience the best of the five senses can drive Taurus natives to connect with anything that makes the physical world come more alive. You are energetically designed to create more beauty, peace, and stability in your life.

Your physical self awakens when you take in messages from the Taurus-ruled parts of your body: throat, thyroid glands, neck, voice, and tonsils. Stay mindful of your sensations in these areas, and stay open to the idea that they can bring signals about physical and emotional challenges that may require more attention or ongoing care.

Taurus energy encourages you to stand firm and strong in yourself without resisting change and growth. All healthy relationships embrace flexibility and evolution, but because Taurus energy can be slow-moving, hesitant, or avoidant at times, you will want to look deeply into what may be driving any unconscious fear of connection. As a Taurus, you need to go at your own pace without feeling rushed. How can you honor the intentionality of this level of patience and determination while staying open to expanding?

As your Taurus energy matures, a new sense of what life means to you will become more important. You may determine what you need to live a good life that is simple, beautiful, and brimming with joy and peace. When you detach from too many external influences and come back into the heart of what you love the most, you access a deep well of inner peace and harmony. It is here that Taurus energy feels safe and secure in this lifetime.

As a Taurus soul, you are awakening to a new sense of security and power within yourself that you can always rely on. You are here to experience the best of the physical world and to enjoy the pleasures of life while staying mindful of what matters to you. As your sense of self-love and self-worth becomes more firmly grounded, you may begin to feel a regular sense of peace and calm that validates who you are in the world.

Blind Spot Energy: Aries (Fire, Cardinal, Masculine)

With your Sun in Taurus, Aries energy may be a blind spot for you if you are not sure what action to take next or if you feel stuck or unable to change. When this happens, it's time to look deep into what drives you. What motivates and inspires your highest good? Once you know that, let Aries' fiery spark support your next steps. Beginning something new or trying something different may also bring you back to yourself. Aries' Fire may not be your natural element, but tapping into it can set you on a new path or keep you going with renewed vigor.

Read the section on the Sun in Aries for more information on the attributes and qualities you may want to keep in your awareness.

Ongoing Development: Gemini (Air, Mutable, Masculine)

Gemini energies urge you to move ideas, thoughts, and perceptions through your mind and throat. If your Sun is in Taurus, Gemini reminds you to express yourself and listen to what you're thinking, whether through journaling, talking to a friend, or just hearing yourself speak. If you cannot see a novel solution, path, or way to do something, allow Gemini's mental energy to support your self-expression. Gemini enjoys change and can adapt to life's unexpected developments. You can trust in a more fluid approach to life, especially if you feel stalled out. Keep the energy moving by talking, typing, and traveling with trust in your own process.

Read the section on the Sun in Gemini for more information on the attributes and qualities you are developing.

Balancing Energy: Scorpio (Water, Fixed, Feminine)

As the sign opposite to Taurus on the zodiac wheel, Scorpio encourages you to find balance by going deeper into what you feel and intuit. While earthbound Taurus finds comfort in what is concrete and knowable, Scorpio energy resides beneath the surface, where your subconscious and your psyche play and learn— in realms you may not understand logically. You can benefit from the balancing power of Scorpio by trusting deep influences and impulses and by opening up to people you trust. You don't have to figure it all out on your own. Scorpio energy can be welcomed in therapists, counselors, healers, and guides that lead you through a transformational process to more self-awareness.

Read the section on the Sun in Scorpio for more information on the attributes and qualities you are balancing.

Sun in Gemini (Air, Mutable, Masculine)

Messenger, Storyteller, Comedian, Teacher, Student, Writer

The soul's intention to be guided by the Sun in Gemini is to experience life with an active, engaged mind that remains open and curious about the world. Gemini souls are often gifted with a high level of mental and verbal acuity, which serves them well in connecting to the people and situations around them.

As a Gemini, you soak up a lot of information everywhere you go, and your keen memory retains details that others overlook. You are highly visual and may also experience heightened listening skills, picking up on what is being communicated very easily. Gemini is associated with our early experiences of learning, studying, writing, and speaking, including primary education, peer groups, and sibling relationships. Your formative years opened you up to a lot of sensations in the physical world and provided questions for you to ponder about life. Gemini energy is curious and open to understanding what is going on in the world, from the mundane to the complex. It picks up on every communication style and idiosyncrasy—verbal expression, physical movements, body language, tone of voice, rate of speech, word choice—and then often remembers it all, down to the tiniest detail.

As Gemini souls travel through life, they may encounter a theme of variety and crave a wide range of experiences at all stages of personal development. The active Gemini mind can get bored with routine, and may explore doing things differently.

Gemini, a masculine energy, is the first Air sign and first mutable sign on the zodiac wheel. Mutable signs are adaptive and lean into transitions, so if this is your sign, you always want to learn new, useful, and insightful information. The fast-moving energy of your body and mind allows you to learn a lot and move forward quickly when you grasp something. You may learn faster and ask more questions than others when you are especially interested in a topic. Then you may have a desire to teach, to write, and to share what you've learned.

Soul Growth in Gemini

As you may gather from its symbol of twins, individuals with the Sun in Gemini often have a theme of duality in their lives. This can show up as a need to learn something twice, as experiencing a lesson twice, or as seeing both sides of the proverbial coin. They may also be drawn to understand things from both right-brain and left-brain perspectives. They may feel as if they are split between two personalities, or two directions, or two points of view, or two differing sides of themselves. This can result in inner conflict, which may show up as anxiety, mental spinning, overthinking, and not knowing how to calm the mind.

If this is your sign, your nervous system may exude this energy as well, through restlessness, shaky hands, or physical twitching. It's vital for you to develop healthy mindfulness habits and physical exercises that move the energy from your mind out through your body. Even better, tie these activities to expressing your thoughts in a way that relieves your overactive mental energy. You remain adaptable and flexible in your approach to gathering more understanding, especially through specifics, details, data, and interesting tidbits of knowledge.

As Gemini souls mature, they may learn to slow down the mental stream of thought and harness how the mind works. Remember, you can stay open to multiple possibilities without feeling as if you have to chase every rabbit down every rabbit hole. When you find yourself becoming overly fixated on details or particulars, step back and see the broader viewpoint. Shift your focus to the bigger picture and explore new ways of approaching a topic.

As a Gemini, you may be a jack-of-all-trades, yet master of none. Your mentally active mind and body lead to many places and experiences, but you also have a restlessness that keeps you moving on. You are energetically designed to be a sprinter who prefers short-term endeavors and ongoing options. You will feel more fulfilled as you gravitate toward more of these scenarios and options in your life. If you are feeling trapped in a job, a relationship, or a lifestyle, it may be because you need variety and excitement. Be careful of hasty decision-making when you desire change, however, and don't throw the baby out with the bath water. You can honor your need for more interesting projects and pursuits without losing what's good about what you have.

You need freedom in many areas of life, as well as people who can give you the room to follow your natural energy and provide space for your restlessness. However, not everyone is wired this way, and you will need to communicate what you want and need in order to maintain healthy relationships and develop ongoing trust. Others can only understand your needs if you share them.

Gemini souls need to stay mindful of when to stop talking and thinking, and when it is more appropriate to listen and slow down. You are learning to be in control of your mind and your quick-moving energies. Guided meditation—when someone narrates a relaxing scene or provides calming imagery—is an excellent tool for consciously directing the mind. You can also relieve mental pressure by tuning in to your body. Slow down and listen to your breathing patterns. Look at where you are holding any nervous energy. Simple practices that guide you into the body will support your energy in wonderful ways.

Your physical self is awakening through messages from the Gemini-ruled parts of your body: hands, fingers, arms, neurological wiring, and lungs. Stay mindful of the energies that you sense in these areas, as they may require more attention or ongoing care.

The Gemini soul is here to master mental energy and to be a powerhouse in communication and intellectual pursuits. Your intellect and your communication style will provide vital resources as you move through life. Pursue various modes of communicating and expand the ways in which you can convey your truth, especially in relationships of all kinds. You are learning to be responsible with your words, mind, and self-expression. While Gemini energy feels comfortable and fulfilled in the mental realm, you can always develop the physical, emotional, and spiritual aspects of your daily interactions as well. You are a full and rich being who brings self-expression, communication skills, and thoughtfulness to all areas of your life.

Blind Spot Energy: Taurus (Earth, Fixed, Feminine)

Taurus energies remind Gemini to slow down and look at what makes practical sense before going off in too many directions at once. If Gemini is your Sun sign, draw on Taurus energies to realistically assess what you can see through to completion, including the time, tasks, and energy involved. Taurus asks you to ground yourself and listen to your body for guidance. With determination, you can carry any idea from a seed to a beautiful manifestation when you take the time to think through the details and assess what is worth your commitment.

Read the section on the Sun in Taurus for more information on the attributes and qualities you may want to keep in your awareness.

Ongoing Development: Cancer (Water, Cardinal, Feminine)

Gemini's active mind does well to drop into the Cancer heart space for deeper understanding of what you need and feel. Cancer's energies ask you to consider what feels good beyond what makes sense intellectually, and to look at what opens up more of your emotional world. As a Gemini, you can develop more fully by integrating the heart into your mental processes. Cancer energy reminds you to practice receiving and caring for yourself when you are busy and active.

Read the section on the Sun in Cancer for more information on the attributes and qualities you may want to keep in your awareness.

Balancing Energy: Sagittarius (Fire, Mutable, Masculine)

While Gemini energy focuses on daily issues and mental pursuits, Sagittarius energy opens you up to the bigger picture of life and the worthwhile experiences that will form and shape you. This energy invites those with the Sun in Gemini to get out of their minds. "Travel beyond what you know," Sagittarius urges. "See something new and expand what's possible for you. Grow through new adventures." The balancing energies of Sagittarius remind Gemini that there is more to understand, study, and see that will keep you invigorated throughout life.

Read the section on the Sun in Sagittarius for more information on the attributes and qualities you may want to keep in your awareness.

Sun in Cancer (Water, Cardinal, Feminine)

Mother, Nurturer, Caretaker, Counselor, Maiden, Family Man

The soul's intention to grow through the Sun in Cancer is to live with an open heart and caring nature while at the same time maintaining healthy boundaries. Cancer souls are energetically tuned in to their immediate environment and the people around them, often picking up on subtle clues and emotional messages. They are learning in this lifetime how to trust what they feel as one of their unique gifts.

If your Sun is in Cancer, you may often feel deeply, or feel moody, or feel private and internal. Cancer energy seeks a safe home environment to turn to for comfort and solace, a place in which to process your inner world and to return to emotional equilibrium. You are gifted with a very open and caring emotional capacity, but this carries with it a responsibility to protect your energy field. You are learning how to care for your softness, which can feel very vulnerable at times. You probably adopted some self-protection strategies at an early age. But embracing vulnerability while maintaining boundaries can lead you to great strength.

Cultural messaging can sometimes tell us to keep a lid on our feelings. Cancer souls may benefit from developing a personal emotional process for moving through their inner world. In this way, they honor themselves. For example, when you are feeling emotionally overwhelmed, sensitive, or defensive, learn to give yourself space and time to ride the waves. Go to a private place—your yoga mat, bedroom, desk, or favorite chair—and allow the truth of your feelings to flow. Honor your emotions as they show up and accept them as temporary messengers. The more you ride these waves, the more you will trust yourself. Working against your feelings or keeping them bottled up will leave you drained and frustrated.

Cancer is a feminine energy, as well as the first Water sign and second cardinal sign on the zodiac wheel, coinciding with the start of summer. As an element, Water has been associated throughout history and across the globe with emotions. Our first emotional experiences in childhood inform lifelong patterns of safety and well-being. Cancer souls experience this at a deep level, with every family member, from siblings to parents, contributing to their initial sense of safety—being seen, being heard, and being acknowledged.

Most Cancer souls are sensitive and highly attuned to the emotions of others, though this may have been misunderstood by their parents or caregivers when they were younger. You may have been told you were touchy, needy, or just "too much." With the right support and tools, however, being sensitive and emotional can be a massive strength and a gift. Many Cancer souls, as well as those with strong Scorpio and Pisces in their astrological charts, may identify as empaths and/or highly sensitive people who feel a lot and unconsciously absorb the energy around them. Again, this can feel like a burden or a strength, depending on how you approach it.

Because they can pick up on subtle energies and care a lot about others, those with the Sun in Cancer are called to be discerning about what they absorb and how they relate to people. You may feel exhausted without knowing why. When this happens, ask yourself if what you are feeling belongs to you or if you have picked up emotions or energies from others. Try visualizing yourself being energetically cleansed by a waterfall or high-frequency light. As you bathe in this sensation of water or light, imagine the energies and emotions of others being lovingly removed from your energy field and returned to their rightful owners. Energy practices like these will fortify your sense of yourself, as well as help you detach from the energies in the world at large.

Soul Growth in Cancer

As your Cancer soul matures, you will develop the capacity to care for others without needing to carry them or mother them. Your unconscious mothering tendencies can feel satisfied when you're giving to others, and you enjoy nurturing and providing for others. People may turn to you for help or when they need a kind listening ear. But you must develop emotional and energetic boundaries that ensure that others remain responsible for themselves—including their choices, their actions, and their feelings. You do not need to be everyone's on-demand caretaker. You do not have to provide support for the whole wide world. Take care of your own needs and heart. Then, from this space, you can show up for others when they appreciate you and are able to give back in equal measure. In this way, you develop your ability to receive. Being able to receive from others allows you to cocreate mutually fulfilling connections, even if it is with only a few select people.

Your Cancer soul is awakening to reciprocity and mutual caring in heart-based connections. You long to connect emotionally with others on common ground so that you can feel peaceful and revitalized. The most fulfilling relationships in your life will honor your sensitivities in a loving way and provide a safe place for you to be your full self. Stay mindful of when you are giving or providing too much as a way to feel loved and validated. Look at how you are caring for others, and assess if the caring is mutual. Your wide-open emotional world and loving heart will provide endless opportunities for developing emotional and energetic boundaries with others throughout your whole life. Practice discernment around whom you trust with your heart, and know that this will take time to learn.

Your physical self is awakening through messages from the Cancer-ruled parts of your body: chest, breasts, womb, stomach, and the physical flows of water and emotions. Stay mindful of the energies that you sense in these areas, as they may require more attention or ongoing care.

You are learning to speak from your heart and to ask for what you need directly. You may assume others know what you're thinking and feeling, or that they are as tuned in as you are to their own feelings, but chances are they are not. Your Cancer soul can be very self-protective, so it is vital to communicate what you're feeling, even if that requires giving yourself time and space to formulate your personal expression. The more you can release and process your feelings internally, the better you will be at sharing them in a clear way. Did you develop defense mechanisms early in life to protect yourself against feeling hurt or vulnerable? Did you shut down your sensitivity to others or within your family dynamics because it didn't feel safe? It is often worthwhile for those with Cancer planets to do personal work around their sensitive or empathic energies so they can learn to feel strong in themselves regardless of what they are sensing in their environment.

If your Sun is in Cancer, you will learn to live from an open heart and to trust what you're feeling. Your emotional world is a significant part of your navigation system, and it will require fine-tuning as you progress on your Cancer journey. Cancer souls are here to experience a whole spectrum of sensations and to love their own sensitivities. You are gifted with a rich experience of life. The more you can harness your energy with consciousness around your own needs, the more awakened you will become to all of the beautiful energies you can truly share and experience with others.

Blind Spot Energy: Gemini (Air, Mutable, Masculine)

Gemini energies remind those with the Sun in Cancer to step away from the emotional world and look for logical understanding as well. Ask questions, gather more information, and be willing to communicate more. Gemini may feel like a blind spot because it is asking you to detach from what you're sensing and look at the facts. When you pay attention to this blind spot, your heart and mind operate as a team, which can help you bring even more dreams to life, to solve problems, and to identify what feels important to you.

Read the section on the Sun in Gemini for more information on the attributes and qualities you may want to keep in your awareness.

Ongoing Development: Leo (Fire, Fixed, Masculine)

Cancer energy becomes stabler as you move into the strength of Leo. Both Cancer and Leo connect to the heart, but the roar of Leo helps you develop pride, courage, and the ability to be more yourself by embracing all your talents. Leo's creative energy gives you confidence to express yourself and put yourself out into the world more. Leo strengthens the soft spots of Cancer and helps you feel powerful in what you want to create and share.

Read the section on the Sun in Leo for more information on the attributes and qualities you may want to keep in your awareness.

Balancing Energy: Capricorn (Earth, Cardinal, Feminine)

Capricorn provides a balancing perspective to Cancer energies by detaching you from what you feel and illuminating where you may be overly subjective. Capricorn brings you out into the real world and asks you to consider what needs to be done for practical gain. When Cancer souls want to hide or stay in a safety zone, Capricorn energy balances these vulnerable qualities with reminders of their strength and fortitude to show up and keep going.

Read the section on the Sun in Capricorn for more information on the attributes and qualities you may want to keep in your awareness.

Sun in Leo (Fire, Fixed, Masculine)

Performer, Creator, King, Queen, Artist, Protector

The soul's intention to experience life through the Sun in Leo is a driving desire to express yourself and create as only you can. Leo's rays of light emanate as the courage to be seen and the confidence to stand alone. Leo souls are developing the ability to rely less on the opinions and feedback of others, while boldly following what calls to them. They may notice a theme in their lives of taking risks to discover their talents and what they want to create with their energy. If this is your Sun sign, you may be drawn to leadership roles as a showcase for your courageous spirit and your ability to take charge. Leo souls are developing pride in a healthy sense of self, but this must be built with a conscious, ongoing awareness of how their energy affects others, including their needs and thoughts. It will feel important to you to express yourself in all areas of life.

Leo is a masculine energy—the second Fire sign and the second fixed sign on the zodiac wheel. When the Sun is in this sign, this creates a roaring blaze of fixed Fire energy, the personification of a midsummer bonfire—celebratory, reliable, strong, and warm, with the will and determination to burn big, high, and wild. Leo souls are gifted with a playful spirit. When young, they run wild and take big risks, sometimes with little regard for the consequences of their actions.

As they mature, Leo souls may develop ways to enjoy fun and games with more discernment, however. They learn to seek fulfillment through joy and by feeling motivated to follow what is pulling at their heartstrings. The inner child of Leo wants to be alive and free. As a Leo, you may feel a rising need to express this part of yourself.

Soul Growth in Leo

Leo souls are developing the confidence to stand strong in themselves. If your Sun is in Leo, you will have opportunities to trust yourself while remaining open to external pressures. Leo can be unconsciously shut down, so you are learning more about how to connect and work with others for mutual benefit. Even though you may want to run the whole show, you need support and help from others at times. You are learning how to share—your toys, your ideas, your possessions, your energy—so that you can give and take mindfully. Leos can hold a sense of entitlement around what they deserve and should receive, so check in with these parts of yourself that seek validation. Give yourself this recognition regularly and remain conscious of when you are looking for it outside of yourself. Envision yourself receiving light and love in your solar plexus. Feel a sense of rising power that is warm, inviting, and joyful. Energetically connect to the blazing Sun when you need confidence, support, and love from the cosmos.

Leo souls are learning to live boldly and courageously through the heart by raising their own consciousness around what it means to give and receive love. You may find yourself in relationships and partnership dynamics that emphasize your deepest needs, whether by meeting those needs or by highlighting what is missing. You can learn to share from an awakened heart. Your Leo nature seeks to protect and honor those you love and to ensure you are feeling recognized and loved in return. Responsible, aware, and fully realized love means trusting that you can give and receive in joyful balance. Stay mindful of any barriers around your heart that may keep people away. Keep your pride in check and learn to adapt and grow. Take personal responsibility and embrace mutual, balanced love affairs. You may face big risks in love, dating, and mating, but you can also find big rewards there as you bring a solid, reliable love forward into these connections.

Leo is comfortable in the limelight and loves being seen. However, stay mindful of how you attract people into your world. Not all attention is good attention. Are you selling yourself out or performing for the applause of others? Are you wearing a false mask so others will accept you or love you? Are you denying your authentic self? Assess how you show up at work, in relationships, in friendships, and in your family life to determine if you are playing a role in any of these areas. Polish up your sense of self from within, without giving too much weight to the perceptions of others.

As Leo souls mature, they often feel a fiery shift into their purpose as their open hearts develop full confidence in their gifts and abilities. When you live with intention and it is felt by those around you, this results in new levels of personal recognition. You can let go of any unconscious need for validation as you find and revel in a stable sense of worth within yourself. Leo energy grows through higher levels of confidence, which you only develop through cycles and phases of risk-taking. This includes the risk and reward of owning yourself as a full and complete being.

Your physical self is awakening through messages from the Leo-ruled parts of your body: heart, chest, solar plexus, and upper back. Stay mindful of the energies that you sense in these areas, as they may require more attention or ongoing care.

Leo energy is gifted with passion and charisma, as well as leadership, personal willpower, determination, and a yearning for deep joy. Follow what calls to your heart. Trust where your desire rises in pursuit of a goal. Your Leo soul can live a very rewarding and inspired life that naturally attracts others with similarly open hearts. As you develop increasing confidence in your abilities, you will also feel higher surges of creativity and self-expression. Leo energy can bring connection and fulfilment to life while allowing others equal space to shine and share.

Blind Spot Energy: Cancer (Water, Cardinal, Feminine)

Cancer energies remind those with the Sun in Leo soul to drop into the softness of their hearts. Your ego may override any expression of vulnerability, but when you turn a listening ear to the quieter messages within, you open up a deeper level of self-knowledge. Cancer is a feminine energy that can sense what is unspoken and wants to connect from a true place. Embracing Cancer's gifts of deep empathy and emotional fluidity can temper your tendency to take charge and take up space.

Read the section on the Sun in Cancer for more information on the attributes and qualities you may want to keep in your awareness.

Ongoing Development: Virgo (Earth, Mutable, Feminine)

If your Sun is in Leo, you can develop by leaning into the mental strengths of Virgo, which bring your attention to the particulars of life and what you are creating. Virgo energy helps refine and sculpt the wild, bold desires of Leo so you can work with a greater focus on a tangible result. Virgo provides realistic feedback and solutions and can help ground you in daily self-care routines that may feel boring or repetitive, but are vital to your well-being and health. Virgo strengths will guide your fiery nature to more satisfying outcomes.

Read the section on the Sun in Virgo for more information on the attributes and qualities you may want to keep in your awareness.

Balancing Energy: Aquarius (Air, Fixed, Masculine)

Aquarius' opposing energies provide a wider viewpoint than the one the self-oriented Leo habitually assumes. Aquarius offers a detached understanding of the Universe that exists beyond the self or the small community. Through

Aquarian energies, Leos consider more feedback and suggestions and tap into the strength of diversity. When you become self-consumed or isolated, Aquarius energies can remind you that the world is a very big place and there are infinite ways to approach a situation or experience. What would you do if you couldn't do anything wrong? When Leo energy is stuck, Aquarius can tap a flow of new ideas and questions to ponder.

Read the section on the Sun in Aquarius for more information on the attributes and qualities you may want to keep in your awareness.

Sun in Virgo (Earth, Mutable, Feminine)
Healer, Craftsman, Analyst, Coach, Body Expert, Specialist

The soul's intention to live through the Sun in Virgo is to combine the body and mind for optimum experiences in the physical world. Virgo gifts include efficiency, responsibility, problem-solving, and healing abilities, as well as the desire to combine and implement these talents to create a satisfying and fulfilling life.

If your Sun is in Virgo, your active mind enjoys puzzles, word games, organizing, crafts, anything that involves using your hands and developing and following a process. The keen Virgo eye spots opportunities for improvement or things that have been overlooked. You can bring new solutions into the world through these observations. Virgo souls find it gratifying to contribute to something greater than themselves, while remaining clear in their individual talents. Virgos thrive in the harmony they can develop between body, mind, and spirit as they focus on a particular craft, talent, skill, or insight. Your daily devotions become ways to structure and experience your world, as these routines refine and honor what you value most.

Virgo gifts include problem-solving, finding hidden solutions, and supporting a process through to completion. Your interest in stress-testing and optimizing processes means you can tweak and improve systems and protocols. As you apply incremental changes, your work and perceptions are increasingly seen and valued by others who struggle to see the details or problems in the ways you can.

Virgo is a feminine energy, as well as the second Earth sign and second mutable sign on the zodiac wheel. Mutable signs tend to be diplomatic, adaptable, and open to possibility. For Virgos, this can manifest as bringing tangible improvements that support a bigger plan or broader change. The Earth energy of Virgo brings grounding and discernment and seeks satisfaction in health and steady progress. Your eye for discovering what could be better, however, can easily flow into a drive for perfection. You may work relentlessly or remain hyperfocused on what can be corrected, edited, refined, or healed. It is important to watch out for times when you are focused on the minutiae to the point that you lose sight of the bigger picture. You may at times get lost in your work or the duties of a particular role, perhaps with an unconscious motivation to demonstrate that you are "good enough" or "perfect."

As a Virgo, your critical eye can lead you to give sharp feedback to others, which may not be your intention. Your perceptions can come across as judgments delivered in a framework of good vs. bad or right vs. wrong. Stay aware of how you communicate and give feedback with an intention of incorporating kindness. Not everyone is looking for solutions or improvements. Your best intentions may be met with resistance or disinterest. You are blessed with a deep intelligence that can pinpoint what others may not notice, and when your message is delivered with higher awareness, you can be a powerful and influential helper.

Soul Growth in Virgo

Virgo energy delights in making daily progress toward a long-term goal or lifestyle habit. The shadow side of this quality can be a tendency to have a harsh inner monologue or unrealistic expectations of what is and is not acceptable. Striving to be better or make improvements can unconsciously drive you to hold yourself to standards that are not sustainable or practical. Monitor messages of guilt or imperfection. If you find you are treating yourself unkindly, remember that you are a human being and you are *enough*.

Your physical self is awakening through messages from the Virgo-ruled parts of your body: stomach, intestines, spleen, digestive tract, and the wiring of your nervous system. Stay mindful of the energies that you sense in these areas, as they may require more attention or ongoing care.

Practice settling your mind to match the tempo of your body's rhythms. You can do this through meditation, yoga, self-hypnosis, or other gentle mind-body practices. When you create an internal harmony between these systems, you'll feel a calming of your mind and your nervous system, a soothing of your digestive tract, and a respite from all your physical energies. Part of your Virgo soul's mission is to maintain a healthy relationship with your body, your health practices, your physical healing routines, and your personal care. Virgo individuals can tune in to the detailed messages coming from their own bodies. Trust this ability in yourself.

Virgos are energetically designed to care for others as much as they care for themselves. Make sure that you include yourself in your daily priorities and routines, however, and not as the last item on your to-do list. By developing your ability to manage and organize what is best for you, you tap into innate healing abilities and self-care practices that will sustain you through life's vicissitudes and seasons of change.

Virgo souls enjoy the patience and wisdom to see through temporary situations and remember what they can take care of today. Making your body a priority will give you more natural energy and help you feel grounded in yourself. Experiment with what sustenance and nutrients your body needs and on what schedule. You benefit from an intimate and knowledgeable partnership with your body in this lifetime. You will awaken to more ways to care for yourself as you combine your physical perceptions with your mental acuity.

As your Virgo energy matures, you connect with perfection in the present moment—in your body, in your mind, and in your environment. When you sense the beauty of what is, you accept life as it unfolds, day by day. Through this understanding, you tap into deeper self-acceptance and peace within your own being. You will continue to see details, untapped potential, and the inner workings of things. But your priorities and perceptions shift as you mature, so that being of service looks different at various stages of life. Your ongoing satisfaction is tied to discovering new ways to offer your skills, talents, and gifts to others, as you practice what it means to live a healthy life in your one special body.

Blind Spot Energy: Leo (Fire, Fixed, Masculine)

Leo energies remind those with the Sun in Virgo to play, to have fun, and to take risks sometimes—even if they are only small ones. Leo's themes reconnect you to your creative passions, which can pull you out of the myopia and burnout you can sometimes face. Remember to look at Leo energies when you are searching for inspiration and motivation for your next project or worthwhile endeavor. You may find that you reconnect to a hobby or passion you enjoyed when you were younger, as your inner child can be more expressive and open in Leo energies without the pressure to do a task perfectly or out of duty.

Read the section on the Sun in Leo for more information on the attributes and qualities you may want to keep in your awareness.

Ongoing Development: Libra (Air, Cardinal, Masculine)

Virgo encourages you to focus on, work with, and fine-tune things that are important to you. Libra energy encourages you to share your efforts with others. Libra progressively develops your Virgo soul by reminding you to ask for help when needed, and to collaborate with others for support and mutual benefit. Libra offers you ease in your interaction with clients, partners, and allies. You do not have to do it all on your own. Others are interested in what you have to say and share. Libra can help you with deals, negotiations, partnerships, and business contracts, and can further connect you with the right people in the right places.

Read the section on the Sun in Libra for more information on the attributes and qualities you may want to keep in your awareness.

Balancing Energy: Pisces (Water, Mutable, Feminine)

Virgo souls can find balance and freedom in the compassion and softness of Pisces energies. Pisces helps you release your grasp on perfection and impossible standards and step away from overworking yourself to extremes. Take a break and trust what you cannot see. Allow your mind to rest and give your body some downtime with a nap or a vacation. Pisces reminds you that there are ways to float through life and that you do not have to direct the outcome all of the time.

Read the section on the Sun in Pisces for more information on the attributes and qualities you may want to keep in your awareness.

Sun in Libra (Air, Cardinal, Masculine)

Peacekeeper, Agent, Diplomat, Judge, Negotiator, Partner

The soul's intention to develop through the Sun in Libra is to experience equilibrium, harmony, and cooperation as main life themes. Those with the Sun in Libra cocreate through relationships and partnerships and by sharing energies that are mutually beneficial for ongoing growth. They are beautifully designed to cooperate, share, exchange, and work with energies outside of themselves, but they can fall into sacrificing their own needs for the sake of connection. Libra souls are learning how to develop and grow harmonious relationships, while also standing in their power as sovereign beings. They seek profound connections with a wide array of people with shared and differing values, needs, and desires. It is easy for Libra energy to attract and connect. So they may find it a challenge to discern which connections to prioritize so that they can focus on relationships based on equity and mutuality.

Libra is a masculine expression, the second Air sign and the third cardinal sign on the zodiac wheel, creating the unique ability to initiate interactions and conversations in the world that can expand ideals, solutions, and potentials. Libra often brings an objective and balancing perspective for consideration. As a Libra, you can step back from big emotions to evaluate what is happening. You can really shine when it comes to people skills, client work, customer service, negotiations, and healthy conflict resolution. You may naturally exude style, savvy, and a peacefulness that others innately sense.

Libra souls are here to maintain an energy of equilibrium as they move through life. However, this balancing energy can also reveal itself through indecision and not knowing which action to take. You may feel paralyzed amid the balance of pros and cons as you determine what to do next in a situation. Your decision-making process may be focused on other people's needs and desires, as you want to create peace and not upset anyone. Yet you are also learning that it is okay to know what is best for you and to take action with that driving intention. You are not responsible for everyone else. Your desire to reduce conflict and maintain the status quo can prove hard to navigate, so relieve your mind of the worries around what others may think or what others will do next. This may take ongoing personal work, but as you practice detaching from what other people need, expect, and want, you are stabilizing your energy in what is best for you as well.

As a Libra, you may feel drawn to diminish your own needs, thoughts, or desires in order to keep the peace in your interactions. But you are learning how to honor what you need and not to hold yourself back. Consider that you can feel secure in the energy container of your own self, while also providing room for others to be themselves. The internal Libra dance works to synthesize these energies so that you claim space for the fullness of who you are. Allow others to honor you as you honor them. Speaking up for yourself and standing in your own energy field is vital to maintaining your inner peace. Coincidentally, it also makes you an even more trustworthy partner and collaborator when you claim your full self.

Libras seek union and cohesion. As you mature, you may notice themes and patterns around pairing and togetherness in all areas of your life. It would be wise to observe the give-and-take of these interactions. What are you receiving in return for what you give? Is there an equal energetic exchange? Relationships teach you about yourself. Thus you may realize that what you are experiencing in another person is, in fact, a reflection of your unconscious self in some way. You may access the truth of others more readily than your own. If you are not feeling fulfilled or satisfied in some areas of life, do you invest in others before turning inward to understand your own wants and needs? When your energy goes out to another, open up to the awareness that they may reflect your own needs, wants, and desires back to you. For example, you may become more in touch with what you truly need after hearing a friend express what they want and need.

You can understand more about who you are through these reflections and contrasts. For example, by tuning in to a friend's problems and underlying values, you may receive a lightning bolt of clarity about whether or not the same is true for you. The contrast may be obvious and may open up a clear path through some unrelated issue that you are experiencing. Libra souls seek out deep conversations and questions, and often gain more knowingness around important matters as they hear and see themselves through the lens of their interactions.

Communication of all kinds is vital to Libra energies. You are a natural at speaking and sharing your thoughts and are inclined to engage others in conversations on a regular basis. People also sense your willingness to listen, and they may feel open and safe with you. Libra souls are amiable, objective, and interested in others, which brings a sense of neutrality and peace to their energy field.

You are also gifted at talking about difficult subjects or approaching touchy topics from a balanced place. You may benefit from ongoing conscious development of your skills in communication, negotiation, presentation, counseling, public speaking, group discussions, moderation, and other areas that involve navigating meaningful connections.

Soul Growth in Libra

Libra souls are learning to be more conscious of their tendency to give away their energy or parts of themselves to others. This can show up as codependence, comparison, and excessive people-pleasing. Consider if you are trying to take on too much in a situation to facilitate peace or harmony, especially if other parties are not taking ownership or connecting with your needs. Are you maintaining a relationship just to be in one, at the expense of your own needs? It will help you to develop the ability to participate in healthy relationships without holding yourself overly responsible for others.

Your physical self is awakening through messages from the Libra-ruled parts of your body: kidneys, lower back, buttocks, endocrine system, and your skin, the body's largest organ. Stay mindful of the energies that you sense in these areas, as they may require more attention or ongoing care.

As Libras mature, they are guided to connect with themselves first in order to foster genuine relationships with people of similar values and relationship maturity. Successful connections in your life will depend on the shared exchange of energy and self-awareness. You are learning to own your whole self—confidently and without holding back who you are in any way. You do not need to accommodate others to the exclusion of yourself. You can challenge the conditioned belief that you are worthy of love only through another. You are awakening to the internal love that you carry with you every day. It is here that you will find the most fulfilling relationships in your life. Your relationship with yourself is primary. The more you grow and love yourself from within, the more you will experience these energies outside of yourself as well.

Blind Spot Energy: Virgo (Earth, Mutable, Feminine)

The practical Virgo energies remind you to get the details and facts straight in order to make the most of what you want to share with others. Virgo is a dedicated worker that brings your attention to how you are spending your energy every day. What can be improved? Are you taking care of yourself enough? This grounding Earth energy will help balance your overactive mind at times, too. Allow Virgo's strengths to guide you with self-care priorities. Your relationships and connections will improve when you listen to and prioritize your own needs.

Read the section on the Sun in Virgo for more information on the attributes and qualities you may want to keep in your awareness.

Ongoing Development: Scorpio (Water, Fixed, Feminine)

The objective perspectives of Libra move into passion and drive when they draw on the following sign of Scorpio. Scorpio energy increases the intensity of your inner emotional experiences and guides you into deeper connections with others—perhaps even a new purpose. Those with the Sun in Libra develop as they tap into more of what they truly feel and need or when they embark on healing any unresolved parts of their energy field. Scorpio energy also supports Libra in decision-making and understanding what it feels like to know others intimately in a vulnerable, open manner.

Read the section on the Sun in Scorpio for more information on the attributes and qualities you may want to keep in your awareness.

Balancing Energy: Aries (Fire, Cardinal, Masculine)

Aries energy reminds you to know yourself as much as you wish to know others. The balancing energy of Aries helps those with the Sun in Libra to get a clear, singular, independent vision for themselves and to stand on their own when they need and want to. Aries can give you strength of purpose when you choose to do something because it feels right for you. That is reason enough to do it. Aries energy reminds your Libra soul that you are an individual first and discourages you from giving too much or being overly invested in others without checking in on your own needs first.

Read the section on the Sun in Aries for more information on the attributes and qualities you may want to keep in your awareness.

Sun in Scorpio (Water, Fixed, Feminine)
Alchemist, Detective, Investigator, Psychic, Psychiatrist, Strategist

Your soul's intention to experience the Sun in Scorpio signals a powerful lifetime of passion, healing, and deep emotional messages that will push you to transform your energy continually into higher expressions. Scorpio energy brings the gift of ongoing alchemy or transformational magic. As you dig into what is happening at deeper levels of your being, you uncover how to make treasure out of your experiences and assets with wisdom and grace. You are here to experience the depths of personal transformation and emotional power with increasing trust in yourself.

Many Scorpio souls come into this incarnation with a desire to follow a passion or energy intensely. You may be called to work as a researcher, a detective, an investigator, an advocate, or some other vocation that involves exploring energies in search of deeper truth and wisdom. You are able to get to the heart of an issue and learn from it, and your ability to do this only grows as you learn to love and accept yourself fully. This makes you able to guide others as well—in roles like therapist, counselor, psychiatrist, healer, or intuitive. Your journey illuminates unconscious desires and brings conscious understanding of what drives you, always with a strong grounding in your profound capacity to feel.

Scorpio is the second Water sign, the third fixed sign on the zodiac wheel, and expresses a feminine energy. Scorpios are determined, committed, and driven and embody a force of emotional energy that can be very powerful—even overwhelming at times. You may recognize that you have intense emotional experiences that you need to process through a kind of metamorphosis. You can process your deep feelings in a healthy way that moves the intense energy and transforms it into an empowering message or wisdom. Unconscious Scorpio energies will seek to off-load these emotions and energies outside of themselves, however, instead of developing the tools to move through them internally. You are learning to trust your intuition and emotional messages while developing skills to channel your strong feelings, reactions, and sensations in useful directions. You can learn to trust the energetic messages you sense, especially those that are not openly expressed or disclosed.

A theme that emerges during the soul's experience in Scorpio involves knowing how to reclaim your power and energy, which you may tend to give away or dissipate into other people and events. Because they are so tuned-in, many Scorpio individuals absorb energies from others—energies that infiltrate their self-worth and their capacity to love themselves fully. This happens in childhood or later life through trauma, abuse, neglect, rejection, or abandonment. As your Scorpio soul matures, you are guided to look inward and examine what was taken from you—what was removed or suppressed so that you could survive or navigate your life circumstances. Your growing consciousness around any harmful people or experiences in your life then leads you back to your own sense of power and self-acceptance. This is deep soul work. You may feel that you are moving and healing through a soul theme that has traveled with you across multiple lifetimes.

Examine how you share yourself with others, and practice how to remain in your truth and power without going to battle. You will have an ongoing theme of how to merge with others in healthy ways—psychologically, emotionally, intimately, financially, physically, and spiritually. You will also want to stay mindful of feeling the lower Scorpio expressions that arise in you—qualities like manipulation, lying, betrayal, power plays, control dynamics, or suppressing parts of yourself in ways that build into unbearable internal pressure. Scorpios can be skeptical and suspicious, not trusting others when something feels off. Trust what you're feeling while also practicing healthy communication. You can share what you're feeling without adding the Scorpio sting that damages or harms others.

Soul Growth in Scorpio

As your Scorpio soul grows, you connect with a deeper sense of personal power that you feel in the core of your being. Your personal alchemy rises in the form of energy and healing tools that you can work with throughout your life to guide yourself and others. Your intentional use of energy and emotions can be one of your greatest gifts as you learn to transform nearly anything into a more healed and loving state. Follow your passions as they arise, even if they are temporary. Trust what is calling to you energetically.

Another main theme in your life will be developing the ability to let go and release—personally, professionally, financially, spiritually, emotionally, and physically. As you alchemize and transform, you will be called to open up new energies and spaces by letting go of what is past. A Scorpio soul can experience this through big professional changes, significant relationship shifts, financial upheavals or abundance, and ongoing turnovers in life. You are learning to let go. Stay mindful of situations in which you hold on to or obsess over these circumstances. You may be seeking to control them in some manner, but you have the option of trusting that everything that empties will be filled yet again with another energy that matches your own transformation process. This can be very intense, as Scorpio souls tend to sign up for a lifetime of experiences that are deeper than those other people may seek out or understand. You will need support at times, which is why it is wise to call on professionals who can help you navigate anything that is stressful or taking an emotional toll on you. Others will show up for you when you allow them into your energy field.

As a Scorpio, you are learning to trust your energy, your emotions, and your intuition as components of your power. You are a force of nature, which comes with the responsibility to manage and maintain that potency. Your Scorpio desires drive you, and you can run over people with your passions. You have the ability to go into many parts of your life with gusto, and this requires that you stay mindful of the ramifications along the way. You do not have to burn bridges or cut people out completely, although this may sometimes be part of your style as you regularly cleanse and purge. Monitor your self-control mechanisms. Pay attention to any addictions or obsessions that show up for you. You always have the choice of redirecting anything that feels as if it has power or control over you. Remember, you are an energy master who can reprogram yourself in healthy ways, even more so with the guidance and support of others.

Your physical self awakens through messages from the Scorpio-ruled parts of your body: reproductive organs, colon, bladder, bowels, and physical transformations like plastic surgery and transplants. Stay mindful of the energies that you sense in these areas, as they may require more attention or ongoing care.

Scorpio souls are here to reclaim all of their energy with a sense of empowerment. Scorpio energy is drawn to deep connections, so how you share your truth with others while loving yourself and acknowledging your own needs is key. You are awakening to the power of your emotional world, your energy messages, and your intuition as you develop greater trust in yourself throughout your life. You are trusting the rhythm of life to support your ongoing growth—constantly and in magical ways. As you do, you will feel and see how deeply loved you are, beyond anything you could have planned for yourself.

Blind Spot Energy: Libra (Air, Cardinal, Masculine)

Libra energies remind Scorpio to step back and examine the world through an objective lens. Consider the other side of the story or situation, and practice emotional detachment. Even though you feel intensely, you will benefit from understanding both sides of an issue and listening to different perspectives. Libra can help you talk through what you're feeling and let you hear yourself speak. You may feel a calming influence as you tap into the gifts of Libra as well, as you can take a step back and see the value in not being overly invested in an experience, relationship, or situation, especially if it is draining your energy.

Read the section on the Sun in Libra for more information on the attributes and qualities you may want to keep in your awareness.

Ongoing Development: Sagittarius (Fire, Mutable, Masculine)

The powerful transformations of Scorpio rise up to a higher place of wisdom through Sagittarius. Because those with the Sun in Scorpio tend to exist in the weeds of emotional experience, Sagittarius energy can help you zoom out to the bigger picture of your life dreams. Sagittarius will also provide the fire to follow what calls to you next, as well as stability to trust the magic that awaits your every adventure. Scorpio souls grow through Sagittarius as they emerge from their own intense feelings and see how strong they are when they partner with spirit or universal life force.

Read the section on the Sun in Sagittarius for more information on the attributes and qualities you may want to keep in your awareness.

Balancing Energy: Taurus (Earth, Fixed, Feminine)

Taurus energies remind Scorpio to relish life's simple joys, especially when you feel pulled under by strife and complication. The grounding Taurus perspective provides practical ways to view a situation; it helps you outline next steps and minimize wasted efforts. Taurus balances Scorpio with the ability to remember you are loved and valued in the world just for being you. Slow down and feel gratitude for what you have, and relish the renewed sense of self and perspective on life this brings.

Read the section on the Sun in Taurus for more information on the attributes and qualities you may want to keep in your awareness.

Sun in Sagittarius (Fire, Mutable, Masculine)
Explorer, Mystic, Guide, Free Spirit, Professor, Seeker

The soul's intention to live through the Sagittarius Sun is to discover higher knowledge, broader self-understanding, and greater wisdom. Sagittarians are open seekers of understanding who feel empowered by the task of putting together the puzzle of their many accumulated perspectives. If this is your sign, you may notice that your life encompasses a wide array of themes, truths, and beliefs that have shifted over time as your spiritual journey has evolved. Sagittarius brings you the optimistic energy of adventure and exploration, and you may find that restlessness can set in when you feel held back or restrained. Freedom is a core life value for you, whether it's the freedom to be yourself and grow throughout your lifetime or the freedom to live life on your own terms without being tethered. This freedom may also be expressed in warmth, humor, and an optimistic outlook.

Sagittarius, a masculine expression, is the third Fire sign and third mutable sign on the zodiac wheel. You embody the spirit of an Olympic torchbearer, determined to travel independently and move across great distances in your life in the name of a cause that feels meaningful to you. Your enthusiastic energy helps you remain open and flexible through the highs and lows that Sagittarians often experience throughout life. Like a torchbearer, you develop trust and faith in yourself through a committed and purposeful journey, and you will find you can also draw on universal energies for stamina and help in navigating your path.

Sagittarius souls seek out and gather wisdom from their wide-ranging life experiences. You may gravitate toward a strong ideology that reflects your personal values and truth. You may be drawn to topics that explore philosophy, education, law, justice, publishing, cultures, religious studies, worldviews, belief systems, or spiritual interests. Sagittarius energy asks the bigger questions: Why am I here? What is my life's purpose? What do I trust? In what do I believe?

As a Sagittarius, you may feel the presence of a bigger energy throughout your life. This connection to universal energies can empower you. As you learn to trust it more, you begin to feel a magical spark of existence animating your daily life. Sagittarius souls often feel a call to explore what is beyond their known reality and to go farther in their knowledge and experiences of the world. They feel an innate need to move—mentally, spiritually, emotionally, and intuitively. They desire growth and expansion at all levels of their being. Sagittarians are often the ones who journey beyond where their family or friends have been—literally or figuratively—and, on this path, they come to know themselves even more. Your restless spirit and search for more powerful magic may propel your quest for self-knowledge and provide new landscapes for personal fulfillment. But as you chase the next horizon, stay mindful of the fact that you will always travel with yourself. Your answers lie *within*. Devote time to listening to yourself, and discover how vast and limitless your internal landscape can be. The external world may appear enchanting, but the magic of life can also be found within.

It is important for Sagittarians to stay mindful of their own opinions and beliefs without expecting others to agree with them or validate them all the time. As a Sagittarius, you can be passionate about any number of topics and ideals and unconsciously expect others to be on the same page. Monitor your assumptions, as well as your judgment of those who differ with you. Consider using these encounters to open your eyes to the systems of right and wrong you were taught as a child. Teachings instilled in you at a young age may no longer apply to you. In fact, you probably have already begun undoing them so that you can determine your truth now. As you mature, you choose what is correct for you and establish your own truth systems that resonate with how you want to create your life.

Stay mindful of the Sagittarius need to do too much or to be excessive. Sagittarius is associated with expansions of all kinds, including overcommitting, overeating, and overdoing to your own detriment. You may not realize how this desire to grow can show up in all areas of your life until you notice a pattern or theme in how you approach decisions or planning. Exaggerations can be common as well. Your desire to "go big" can make you appear like the life of the party, but it can also portray you as the person who tells the biggest tales and magnifies reality.

Soul Growth in Sagittarius

Sagittarius energy is the great traveler of the zodiac. If this is your Sun sign, you are willing to go far and wide in search of new meaning and new ways of living. You are open to voyaging through every section of the library to discover new areas of research and knowledge to consume. Sagittarians desire an ongoing expansion of body, mind, and spirit. What inspires you to live a bigger experience? This endless searching and willingness to go farther can also lead to a sense of alienation at times. You may feel that you are the only one who sets out in new directions and leaves the pack behind. While you are comfortable being independent and following your own guidance, seek out others of like mind and similar spirit with whom you can share your discoveries. Isolation or loneliness can catch up with you when you leave behind others who hold a truth or beliefs that no longer resonate for you. As you continue to grow, you may experience these types of changeovers in your life regularly. You may outgrow friends, family, or people in your life as you go beyond their areas of interest or their scope.

You may even find it difficult to stay paired with one person longterm because of the speed of your growth and your ongoing personal evolution.

Your physical self is awakening through messages from the Sagittarius-ruled parts of your body: hips, legs, thighs, sciatic nerve, liver, and the body's weight, especially if it fluctuates. Stay mindful of the energies that you sense in these areas, as they may require more attention or ongoing care.

As Sagittarius souls mature, they learn to stay open to differing opinions, ideas, perspectives, truths, political positions, and ideologies. You see the value in the full range of human experiences, and you can tap into the gifts and growth within them all. You are awakening to the unlimited potentials and possibilities that exist in the world, and you are trusting what energetically calls to you at different stages in your life. As you evolve, you become a wisdom-keeper who senses the immense wonder of the world and sees the mystical energy that exists at every level of consciousness.

Blind Spot Energy: Scorpio (Water, Fixed, Feminine)

The energy of Scorpio reminds Sagittarians to connect with a passion before taking off on their next adventure down the open road. Scorpio values deep connection with others, honesty, and knowledge of your emotional needs and your vulnerabilities. You can go deeper in your self-awareness through these gifts when you open up into your heart's needs and the emotional undercurrents that guide you. Scorpio energies remind you to trust yourself. They teach that you can discover even more about your truth through intimate bonds with trustworthy individuals.

Read the section on the Sun in Scorpio for more information on the attributes and qualities you may want to keep in your awareness.

Ongoing Development: Capricorn (Earth, Cardinal, Feminine)

With your Sun in Sagittarius, your accumulation of knowledge, experiences, and perspectives takes concrete form through ongoing development into Capricorn. Capricorn is gifted with organizing, managing, and providing structure to what Sagittarius has discovered and learned, revealing what you can do with the information in a practical manner. The Earth energy of Capricorn gives direction and form to Sagittarian ideals, while also requiring refinement and a reality check. Capricorn energy may provide insight about your professional development or show you how to use your Sagittarius energy in a solid way.

Read the section on the Sun in Capricorn for more information on the attributes and qualities you may want to keep in your awareness.

Balancing Energy: Gemini (Air, Mutable, Masculine)

Gemini energies provide the gifts of conversation, specifics, and thought-provoking questions to the roaming Sagittarian spirit. You are balanced through the Gemini ability to think through what you're following, as well as talk it out with others you trust. Gemini looks for how the pieces will line up and work together, which supports organizing what needs to be done to ensure you don't miss a single detail. Think of Gemini as providing the small print to the large font of Sagittarian ambitions.

Read the section on the Sun in Gemini for more information on the attributes and qualities you may want to keep in your awareness.

Sun in Capricorn (Earth, Cardinal, Feminine)

Administrator, Elder, Mentor, Executive, Wizard, Entrepreneur

Your soul's intention to experience the energies of the Sun in Capricorn is to master all energies in your life diligently and with the desire to make a worthwhile contribution to the world. You may be the person in your family who is driven to go farther, build something important, push the limits of success, or

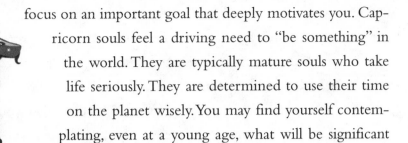

focus on an important goal that deeply motivates you. Capricorn souls feel a driving need to "be something" in the world. They are typically mature souls who take life seriously. They are determined to use their time on the planet wisely. You may find yourself contemplating, even at a young age, what will be significant and purposeful for you to pursue in this lifetime.

Capricorn is an ambitious energy that can responsibly handle hard work, challenges, burdens, and the rewards that come from seeing a goal through to completion. In your life, the Sun in Capricorn will motivate you to follow a goal, a plan, a business, or a passion that can bring about very satisfying levels of success and achievement. You are designed to be seen and recognized for your hard work and your long-term efforts, which gives you a unique stamina and influence in the world.

As a Capricorn, you are strong, capable, and gifted with keen perceptions. You are a dedicated worker when you are following a passion or life path that allows you to apply your talents, your knowledge, and your leadership abilities. Capricorn energies gravitate toward positions of authority. You can handle a lot of information, plans, ideas, and potentials and then channel them into one strategic direction. It is important for you to have an area of your life that allows your strengths to come alive and be recognized. Capricorn souls often apply their skills and talents for the benefit of others by building or contributing to an organization, a business, or an institution.

Starting at a young age, many Capricorn souls tend to feel responsible for more than just themselves and will take on what needs to be accomplished, especially in the family. Capricorns are often serious-minded; they hold themselves and others accountable. They are gifted with managing, supervising, producing, and working hard to achieve results. These innate energies can show up within your family life by identifying you as the one who directs others, including your own parents, and ensures that no obligations are forgotten. You may have had chores, a job, or an internship that allowed you to demonstrate your competence at a younger age than most of your peers. Early life experiences may have opened you up to the world at large and planted seeds around what you wanted to be "when you grew up." This then gives you a goal to work toward, no matter how much time, energy, or effort is involved. This helps you define your life purpose.

Capricorn, a feminine expression, is the third Earth sign and the fourth cardinal sign on the zodiac wheel. Your dedication and drive bring about tangible lifestyle achievements. You are driven to identify the bigger picture of your life and to make the most of your time on the planet through industrious, useful contributions. Many Capricorn souls are entrepreneurial, business-minded, and motivated to assess their personal position in the community. As an Earth sign, Capricorn knows that results matter and you can handle the challenges that arise during long-term climbs to the top—whatever that means to you personally. You take your time to do things right.

Your Capricorn energy needs goals and a direction to follow, however, or else you can feel lost and may be hard on yourself for not doing enough. You may hold yourself to unrealistic expectations at times, often from the internal pressure to do something useful for the world at large. You are learning that it is okay to take breaks, to go on vacation, and to step away from the workplace. Listen to yourself. You may realize that there is another direction or goal that is in better alignment with what you want as your personal consciousness grows. You don't have to hold yourself to high standards if your heart's not in the work. Remember to check in with what you want and what makes you happy to determine what is worth your time, energy, and attention. Too often, you can be working away on something out of a sense of obligation, and then realize you've lost a piece of yourself along the way because you're overly identified with external appearances or acclaim from others. Take time to ask if you're seeking recognition only from others, or if you're also allowing room to recognize your own personal needs and desires.

Soul Growth in Capricorn

As your Capricorn soul matures, you may reassess what is worthwhile and important in life. You are learning to listen to yourself more, to give yourself downtime. You don't have to take on all of the responsibilities of life, especially things that other people should do for themselves. You do not need to hold up the world. Being driven, determined, and relentless is not the only way to live. What brings you joy and happiness? Where do you feel a lightness in your body and a freedom in your soul? Monitor whether the burdens of the world are weighing too heavily on you, and step back when needed.

You are also learning that it is okay for other people to take care of you. You can trust others to show up for you, but you need to be open and allow them to do so in a way that may be different from yours. Assess whether your need to maintain control is grounded in necessity, survival, unconscious programming, or a fear that everything is going to fall apart.

Capricorn souls who don't have a designated "title" in a job or career are here to organize and manage their own energy for maximum satisfaction and results in life. You may be managing or in charge of something simply because you have gravitated toward it—household needs, school events, extracurricular activities, community groups, neighborhood priorities, and any other decision-making authority roles.

Capricorns often become fantastic mentors, guides, experts, and teachers. Your natural leadership capacity provides guidance for others to learn from and follow, especially after years of dedicated service or work in your chosen field. You demonstrate how to take on commitments. You are living proof that long-term energy pays off with continued patience and applied effort.

Your physical self is awakening through messages from the Capricorn-ruled parts of your body: knees, spine, lower back and lumbar support, teeth, and the body's overall bone structure. Stay mindful of the energies that you sense in these areas, as they may require more attention or ongoing care.

With a Capricorn Sun, you are gifted with energetically structuring your life for success, even if it takes a while to figure out what that looks like for you. You are determined, ambitious, and strong. These Capricorn energies are needed in the world to provide ongoing direction, fortitude, and achievement. You demonstrate how life rewards us over time, as well as how we show up on a daily basis in ways that are vital for long-term success.

Blind Spot Energy: Sagittarius (Fire, Mutable, Masculine)

Sagittarian energies remind Capricorns to stay open to the bigger picture of life and to make time for fun. The light of Sagittarius brings warmth, humor, and a positive spin to whatever you may be moving through and supports you in stepping back from being too hard on yourself or expecting too much. Capricorn souls can be very focused on what needs to be done, so Sagittarian themes can help you open up to more possibilities and to the power of unseen energies at work. You may gain new understandings around your life, your goals, and your current priorities when the Sagittarius spirit returns you to the multiple experiences and adventures you can explore in the world.

Read the section on the Sun in Sagittarius for more information on the attributes and qualities you may want to keep in your awareness.

Ongoing Development: Aquarius (Air, Fixed, Masculine)

Your Capricorn energy develops through Aquarius by taking your work, your ideas, and your knowledge to a bigger audience or world. Aquarius is the energy of diversity, humanity, and cocreation with others for a new outcome. You are learning to work toward common goals with others. You are discovering what it means to talk out issues and problems authentically, even when you're not in charge or the final decision-maker. Capricorn souls grow through the new innovations and solutions that Aquarius offers. After all, you could not have arrived at this same place on your own. Community matters, and you can feel supported in a whole new way through these connections.

Read the section on the Sun in Aquarius for more information on the attributes and qualities you may want to keep in your awareness.

Balancing Energy: Cancer (Water, Cardinal, Feminine)

Cancer energies balance Capricorn by offering a softer perspective and inviting you to tap into your own needs. What are you feeling and sensing in yourself and others? Cancer reminds you to turn inward and to take care of yourself, even though you may be focused on the next deadline to be met or the next project that needs to be accomplished. Think of Capricorn as the workweek and Cancer as the weekend, when you can take a break and relax your shoulders. Rest, relaxation, and downtime provide pleasure and renewed vigor for Capricorn's diligent pursuits.

Read the section on the Sun in Cancer for more information on the attributes and qualities you may want to keep in your awareness.

Sun in Aquarius (Air, Fixed, Masculine)

Genius, Inventor, Visionary, Humanitarian, Rebel, Scientist, Activist

Your soul's intention to experience the energies of the Sun in Aquarius draws you to follow a guiding vision that fulfills your own unique spark of brilliance. You arrived with a deep internal desire to do something different and fascinating in this lifetime that would allow for freedom, independence, creativity, and self-expression on your own terms. Aquarius souls hold a desire to contribute to the bigger picture with their accumulated knowledge, while intentionally applying what they've learned in useful ways. With your Sun in this sign, you may find yourself searching for how to participate in the world in a significant way or how to combine your many talents into something you can offer. You may look for ways to take a potential and make it real for yourself. Because Aquarius enjoys the gift of access to a variety of energy streams and potentials, you are on a journey of self-discovery as you decide which path to follow. You may appear rebellious, radical, or offbeat to those who assume you should follow a more conventional path.

Many Aquarians feel out of place or different from their peers. You are learning about individuality in this lifetime and may notice that your life experiences seem to set you apart from others in some way. You are further developing the ability to trust your own energy field and not to be afraid to go it alone at times to see what you can discover along the way. Aquarius energies often feel very connected to other dimensions, other realms, and other realities that are "out of this world," which makes you appear singular and perhaps ahead of the curve at times. You may find a specialty or passion that lights you up and opens a whole new arena of knowledge for you. One of the ways Aquarians contribute to the world is by doing something new, something special or appealing, something that opens a pathway for others to follow. You can go out into these new areas and bring back what you experience to others—your family, your networking group, your friends, or your online community.

Aquarius, a masculine expression, is the third Air sign and the fourth fixed sign on the zodiac wheel. Masculine signs tend to push forward through action, while Air is associated with the mind and thought. The fixed energies are what motivate you to latch on and stay focused, perhaps with less interest in other people's thoughts or ideas. This energy combination is gifted with the ability to hold ideas, thoughts, and potentials that align you with a higher vision of who you are in the cosmos, and this can propel you to experience many new soul adventures in this lifetime. You are designed to share your individual energy with multiple people through friendships, connections, and relationships. This sharing process helps further refine who you are and determines your style. Aquarius is inquisitive and intelligent, often needing to understand concepts at a deeper level and to see the full spectrum of how things connect and work together. Your mind can grasp many concepts, requiring you to roam mentally when something sparks your interest.

Aquarians may feel resistance to authority, to taking direction, and to following along with a crowd when their energy is not connected to external guidance. Since they can be very clear and determined in what is correct for them, they can shut down outside opinions or perspectives. But you are learning to be mindful of your rebellious nature and not to view others' opinions as a personal affront or as an infringement of your sovereign rights. As you search for a group with whom to connect, you may need to stay aware of what it means to be a part of something bigger than yourself without losing yourself along the way. You can be very strong in yourself without pushing away others or deciding you must do everything on your own terms. Stubbornness and being too rigid can create havoc, whereas cooperation and community may support you in the long run. Determining how to do your own thing in your unique manner within the constructs of the world at large will be one of your life themes and an important area of personal development.

Soul Growth in Aquarius

Many Aquarius souls are looking to belong to something bigger than themselves in order to generate and experience collective energy. You may have a large group of friends and acquaintances who are located all over the world; you may find yourself drawn to online communities or social media. You are energetically designed to share and interact with the world, although you can also be particular about where you spend your energetic resources. Follow your passions and interests to find your relationships. Aquarians tend to need their own space and independence, however, so this may be why you prefer to keep your distance until you are sure you want to participate. These connections will be the most satisfying for you when you can come and go as you please, while also trusting that you have a reliable place for your unique self-expression.

Your physical self is awakening through messages from the Aquarius-ruled parts of your body: ankles, nervous system, circulatory system, and neurological programming. Stay mindful of the energies that you sense in these areas, as they may require more attention or ongoing care.

As Aquarian souls mature, they start to embrace what makes them different and special in the world, especially if these are qualities in themselves that felt unacceptable when they were younger. With your Sun in Aquarius, you may come to understand your perceived faults as beautiful soul gifts that guide your journey of individuation. Aquarius energies can be misunderstood and misinterpreted, however. You are often ahead of the masses and may feel as if you do not belong anywhere. Part of your soul growth is in creating exactly the space you need for yourself first, and then preparing room for others to join you if they hold the same values, intentions, and vision.

Blind Spot Energy: Capricorn (Earth, Cardinal, Feminine)

Capricorn energies help to bring Aquarians back into their internal sense of authority. They remind you to examine how you are showing up in the world and encourage you to honor your commitments. Stay focused on what you want to accomplish, knowing that hard work pays off with Capricorn integrity. You may benefit from realistic feedback and assessment of what matters to you for the long term. Aquarius souls can connect with Capricorn's strength in developing slowly and building for maximum payoff. Capricorn can also ground your ideas in a creative enterprise or business endeavor.

Read the section on the Sun in Capricorn for more information on the attributes and qualities you may want to keep in your awareness.

Ongoing Development: Pisces (Water, Mutable, Feminine)

The mentally strong Aquarius energies begin to soften and dissolve through Pisces' influence. Pisces can help you let go and step back from the world, as well as encourage you to consider how you are able to lighten up your grip on priorities and connections. Everything changes form in life, and the Pisces spirit reminds you to trust in the magic of what you do not yet know. Pisces themes help you detach from rigid expectations or requirements you may have for yourself or others. Then grace can flow in and give you new opportunities to practice trust in a grand process.

Read the section on the Sun in Pisces for more information on the attributes and qualities you may want to keep in your awareness.

Balancing Energy: Leo (Fire, Fixed, Masculine)

Leo energies remind Aquarius souls to come back to their personal energy field for stability, answers, and strength. The fire of Leo balances your Aquarian mental energies, especially when you are too much in your head and not listening to your heart. Tune in to your creative passion on your own terms. Remove yourself from the world and your friends to hear what feels correct for you. Give yourself downtime to feel inspired and motivated from a genuine place that honors what you want as well.

Read the section on the Sun in Leo for more information on the attributes and qualities you may want to keep in your awareness.

Sun in Pisces (Water, Mutable, Feminine)

Dreamer, Artist, Mystic, Healer, Spirit Guide, Therapist

Your soul's intention to move through the energies of the Sun in Pisces is to experience a mystical, trusting understanding of who you are by developing a spiritual perspective on life and of yourself. Pisces souls are here to apply spiritual wisdom and higher understanding to their life experiences, while rising above the limitations of the personal ego. You may feel connected to the whole world at times, and yet you are learning how to know yourself as a unique being who senses and intuits energy at multiple levels of your being. There will be many areas of your personal identity and ego to explore, coupled with a sense that you do not know who you are or where you belong because you float through the real world. Pisces souls are chameleons who can blend in and become what is needed wherever they may be, yet this comes with the responsibility to uncover their individual truth. You are learning what it means to have a strong sense of self while also detaching from the ego's desires.

As a Pisces, you are gifted with a compassionate, kind nature that wants to support and help others. Since you are a natural giver, you will want to monitor how much you offer people and ensure that you are not depleting yourself. Pisces souls can put themselves last on the list and then run out of energy and feel exhausted.

Those with the Sun in Pisces are learning to develop strong boundaries in every area of life. Since you easily absorb emotions, thoughts, and energies at work and at home, it is vital for you to develop tools that keep tabs on and honor your own thoughts and feelings. You may need to develop practices and processes that allow you to step into your own space to contemplate what is true for you. Pisces energy needs privacy and time alone to hear what is essential.

Tell people you need this space. These boundaries will help you handle what is happening around you.

Pisces souls are typically sensitive at many levels of their being—from emotional and physical states, to dietary processes, to unspoken communications between people. You are gifted with intuition, potential psychic abilities, and spiritual talents. Pisces loves existing in other realms, so you may also be drawn to roles that involve metaphysical studies, artistic and creative expressions, music, and fantasy worlds. These are wonderful places to trust yourself when you feel your energy rise in response to something that calls to you.

When the heaviness of the real world and everyday commitments weighs you down, however, you may notice that you prefer to disappear, drift away, or escape your responsibilities. Pisces energy can be restless, unreliable, flaky, and inconsistent. You may need help grounding and applying ongoing effort to what you need to take care of, especially when it comes to commitments to others who are relying on you. One way to approach this is to observe your patterns so you can work with your natural energy instead of against it. For example, you may need a work environment where you have freedom, privacy, and an opportunity to get things done on your own schedule. This can protect you from your own tendency to run away or hide when you feel you're being micromanaged.

As a Pisces, one of the main themes in your life will be to honor your emotional messages and trust that what you feel is correct for you. You may often sense something before it shows up in tangible form. By developing a strong connection with spirit—or god, or a primal source, or the Universe, or your higher self—you can bring comfort to your everyday experiences. You may often tap into energies in the higher realms, especially while you sleep. Once you feel something in your energy field and body, your task is to trust in yourself and what you cannot see. Your intense sensate abilities are a beautiful gift you possess, but they also require ongoing practice and responsibility.

Soul Growth in Pisces

As Pisces souls mature, they learn how to manage their energy effectively and responsibly. This includes their emotional, spiritual, financial, and physical energy. You will have many opportunities to practice speaking up for yourself. It may be difficult at first, but it is essential for your own self-care. Practice a few simple go-to phrases that will give you space and time as needed. *I will need to get back to you on that.* Or: *I am going to think about it before deciding.* Or: *I need some space and time right now before we do anything else.* The more you practice expressing what you need, including the need to be left alone when appropriate, the more harmonious you will feel in your daily experiences. Honor your sensitivities as an empath, an intuitive, and a highly sensitive person.

Many Pisces souls are here to experience karmic themes and energetic completions that require forgiveness, compassion, kindness, and a higher spiritual understanding. You may feel the lower expressions of this energy as victim-consciousness, self-pity, blaming others, or feeling helpless at times. Each of these feelings is an invitation to view yourself in more powerful ways and to understand what you are learning. You are very powerful, even when you rest in a momentary illusion of disconnection and blame. Stay mindful of when your energy sinks and of any unconscious loops in which you may find yourself circling. You will probably benefit from daily energy-clearing processes to remove anything you've absorbed that is not yours. Guided meditations or a mindfulness practice will also help you tune in to more of what is best for you.

Your physical self is awakening through messages from the Pisces-ruled parts of your body: feet, toes, lymphatic system, immune system, and overall body hydration. Stay mindful of the energies that you sense in these areas, as they may require more attention or ongoing care.

Your life will take on more meaning and feel more satisfying when you have a spiritual understanding that resonates with you. You can then go to this higher awareness when the hardships of life or karmic themes show up, and you will gain perspective on what you're truly feeling and experiencing.

Pisces souls are learning to master both the spiritual and physical worlds simultaneously in this lifetime. You are awakening to your energy gifts, your spiritual talents, and your innate ability to trust yourself at a very deep level of your being. You will experience cycles of energy that are bigger than your individual ego needs, requiring you to surrender and let go of what you want in the moment as another manifestation comes in and takes shape. Your ability to be detached and remain in your spiritual power will be one of your greatest strengths.

Blind Spot Energy: Aquarius (Air, Fixed, Masculine)

Aquarius themes remind Pisces souls to consider multiple approaches and angles as they follow their creative inspirations. The strong mental energies of Aquarius can help with problem-solving, talking through concerns or worries, and connecting with others for support. You are never truly alone, and Aquarius will open you up to even more people and groups who are on the same wavelength you are. Allow these Aquarian energies to provide clarity and direction when you feel lost. Tune in to new ways to trust yourself as you begin to see new possibilities that may previously have been hidden. Aquarius can give you breakthrough understandings in an instant.

Read the section on the Sun in Aquarius for more information on the attributes and qualities you may want to keep in your awareness.

Ongoing Development: Aries (Fire, Cardinal, Masculine)

Pisces souls have the opportunity to develop by embracing the Aries spirit of independence, freedom, and following their unique path. Aries energies will remind you of who you are as an individual, and that it is wonderful to know more about yourself as your life unfolds. Pisces energy can feel lost and uncertain at times, but Aries themes involve following what calls to you and trusting your-self above all else. You will develop a stronger self-identity and an ability to be on your own as Aries energies help with your confidence and courage. You may even feel a rising excitement and spark for doing something completely new and different.

Read the section on the Sun in Aries for more information on the attributes and qualities you may want to keep in your awareness.

Balancing Energy: Virgo (Earth, Mutable, Feminine)

Pisces souls benefit from the grounding influence of Virgo and enhance their productivity through focus on the daily details of life. When you feel over-whelmed or confused, allow the balancing Virgo energy to show you exactly what needs to get done today, and only today. Virgo will bring you back into your body and help you discern what is worth your energy right now. Even small steps count. In fact, taking the next smallest step may be your most power-ful tool for success. As a Pisces, you can experience calm and feel more centered when Virgo energies guide you along a process and remind you that there is a solution for everything.

Read the section on the Sun in Virgo for more information on the attributes and qualities you may want to keep in your awareness.

PART TWO

Your Moon Sign

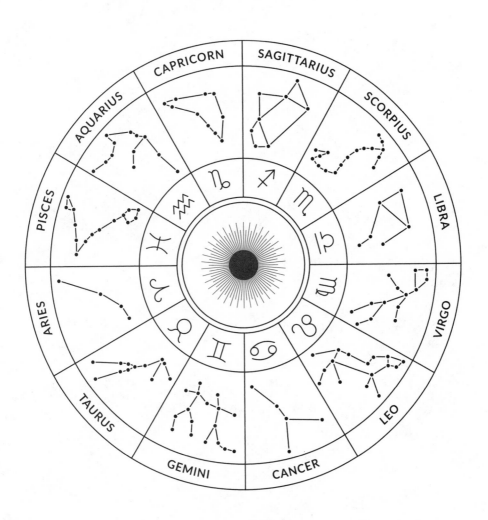

Chapter 3

Lunar Energies

For as long as humans have gazed at the heavens, the Moon has been a constant source of fascination and inspiration. We track its changes and cycles, marveling as it hides and reveals itself. We sense wonder as it passes through phases of dark and light, moving into fullness and falling back into darkness, only to be reborn again. We have long associated the Moon with feminine energy and cycles, with the ocean and the tides, and with the unseen power of night. The Moon guides our patterns of seeking and releasing and presides over our feelings and our emotional needs.

Lunar flows connect you to an energetic process of ongoing self-discovery through the Moon's transitions from light to dark every month. The energy of the Moon ebbs and flows as it moves into a new astrological sign every two and a half to three days—changing clothes, so to speak. In congruence with the Moon's phases, your natal Moon sign transitions into a new field of emotional experiences, intentions, and interpretations of daily life.

In simple astrological terms, your Sun sign is your life force—your sense of self and how you identify your individual talents in this life. Your Moon sign, on the other hand, reminds you that not everything is what it seems. The receptive Moon embraces your feminine nature, no matter what your gender expression, and balances your ego and your reliance on the external world. The Moon reminds you to return to your intuitive messages and your private inner space for guidance and wisdom.

Your Moon sign occupies a central role in your natal astrology chart, because it reveals your internal world, your unconscious needs, your emotional experiences, and your daily perceptions. By understanding your natal Moon as the next layer of astrological complexity, you can gain insight into your daily emotional life and the ocean of feelings we all experience each day. Your Moon sign also provides a lens through which you perceive and experience intimacy in your life, including how you connect with other people and how you share yourself on a more personal level. The first impression you make on others may be a reflection of your Sun sign, but when people are getting to know you more deeply, they are meeting your Moon sign's energies, needs, and private emotions. The Moon invites you to tap into your innermost self, and to reflect your desires through daily expressions. Its energies expose your true heart and sincere feelings, whether they are hidden or on full display.

The Maternal Connection

Your Moon sign is calculated according to the time and place of your birth. The time of your birth is significant because it is the energetic entry point you made into the world when you left your mother's warm womb and became a separate being. When you physically moved out of a comfort zone of nourishment to experience life on your own, your independent existence began.

The moment you left your mother's body was also energetically significant in terms of how you experienced your birth emotionally. This was, among many other sensations and emotions, an experience of separation for you both. The experience of giving birth may have involved a lot of complex feelings for your mother—from joy and exhilaration to grief or depression.

Astrologically, your natal Moon reveals the ways in which your mother felt emotionally and physically during her final days and hours of pregnancy. It may also reflect how you felt during your own birth process. You have no conscious memory of your birth, of course, but the tone of the event nonetheless imprinted you for life. Was it smooth and easy? Was your mother physically ready for your arrival and feeling powerful in her body's ability to give birth? Or was she nervous and uncertain about the end of her pregnancy? Were there any medical complications or unforeseen emergencies that arose as you were about to enter the world?

When the umbilical cord was cut, the physical attachment between your body and your mother's body was severed and you were released to become a separate living being. In much the same way, your Moon sign represents the energetic emotional transfer you shared with your mother as you left the safety of her body and entered the world as a vulnerable, naked child. Of course, both your physical and emotional needs were tied to your mother and/or other caregivers for long after that moment. And knowing more about your Moon sign energies can help guide these ongoing relationships.

Your natal Moon reveals the energy of your initial entry into the world, including how your mother was feeling and what you experienced during your first breaths of life. Because it reveals deep insights into this maternal connection, we are often rewarded with a profound sense of who we are when we become conscious of this part of our self-identity.

As you grow in personal consciousness, you may pick up more ways of getting to the heart of these imprints that have tied you energetically to your mother and to your early life experiences of her. Understanding the natal Moon signs of any siblings you may have can also yield interesting insights. The experience of each birth may have been vastly different between children, and this can open up new perspectives into your ongoing family relationships.

You can also apply this energetic understanding of the Moon to your own children, whether you gave birth to them yourself or not. Knowing your children's Moon signs is a wonderful way to bring clarity about what they need to feel loved, heard, and understood. Their Moon signs can thus be a powerful parenting tool, especially if you have multiple children and you find yourself trying to figure out their individual needs. One child's natal Moon may crave ongoing stimulation and activity (Air signs and Fire signs), while another's may need more quiet time, more privacy, and a slower life pace (Earth signs and Water signs).

Dancing with the Moon

Your lunar energy tends to be subjective, connected with your personal interpretations. For this reason, I think of working with your astrological understanding of this celestial body as "dancing with the Moon." You can dance with your Moon sign more intimately by working with emotional tools, rituals, and therapeutic processes that support hearing its messages and trusting what you feel.

As we've discussed, at first glance, astrology can provide a general understanding of your life's purpose and path. But as you dig deeper into your specific Sun and Moon energies, you discover layers of complexity and specificity. We typically think of the Sun as masculine energy and of the Moon as feminine energy, yet your chart contains multiple manifestations of both these energies. For example, if your Sun is in a feminine astrological sign, and your Moon lives in a masculine astrological sign, these combinations may inform how you understand the feminine and masculine aspects within you. Or you may have both Sun and Moon in masculine signs, or both in feminine signs. Whatever your natal signs, your Sun and Moon inform how these two parts of you ultimately work together, and their energetic combination provides fertile ground for harmonious soul growth. The more you know and understand about your Sun and Moon signs and their elements and aspects, the more you will understand your own needs and who you are in this lifetime.

Lunar energies relate to a part of yourself that only you really know. They speak to the most intimate, lifelong relationship you will ever have—your relationship with yourself. They shape your own emotional imprint. As such, learning more about your Moon sign can be a self-validating astrological practice. Only you can verify what has shown up on your journey and in your world—how you have behaved, what your intentions have been, and what has come out of you.

Your natal Moon determines the principal energy that comes forward in your personal relationships. Successful close relationships involve revealing more about our intimate needs and emotional worlds, which is essentially the same as getting to know one another's Moon signs. Your natal Moon reflects the internal energy you bring to your daily life. When you live with someone, when you interact with friends and family and colleagues, when you share yourself and others do the same, you are sharing your lunar energies. So when you build your understanding and acceptance of your Moon sign, you set yourself up for more successful relationships, for deeper emotional bonds. You achieve more emotional satisfaction, more harmony, more recognition, more security. In short, you acquire an overall understanding of how you move through life.

Your natal Moon also highlights what feels like home to you—emotionally, physically, spiritually, and energetically. Your Moon's sign element (Earth, Air, Water, Fire) may correlate to the types of environments in which you prefer to live. It may influence your innate feeling of home, your preferred comfort zone, and how you choose to decorate your living space so that it feels ideal and safe to you. Here are a few of the hallmarks of the home energy of each element and their Moon signs.

- *Moon in Earth signs (Taurus, Virgo, Capricorn):* natural elements, quiet, solitude, grounded, simple, nourishing, any type of Earth element, including gardens, grass, flowers, herbs, forests, rocks, plants, trees, mountains, etc.

- *Moon in Air signs (Gemini, Libra, Aquarius):* stimulation, connection, information, interactions, communications, any type of Air element, including open-air space, decks, patios, high-level views, many windows, beautiful vistas, etc.

- *Moon in Water signs (Cancer, Scorpio, Pisces):* flow, inspiration, receptive space, peacefulness, any type of Water element, including rivers, lakes, pools, oceans, koi ponds, waterfalls, fountains, bathtubs, etc.

- *Moon in Fire signs (Aries, Leo, Sagittarius):* action, movement, daily activity, inspiration, warmth, any type of Fire element, including city lights, candles, bonfires, firepits, lanterns, decorative lights, tiki torches, etc.

Just as the Moon moves through its phases of illumination every month, you may experience new revelations around your inner world—your deeper feelings and your emotional world—as you move through life. Your Moon sign offers an ongoing exploration of moving from unconscious personal needs to fuller self-awareness, which can also show up in healthier relationships and living in a more satisfying way.

As you dance more intimately with your lunar energies, you may also discover deeper layers of wisdom and knowledge around your energetic connection with your biological mother.

Chapter 4

The Twelve Moon Signs

The Moon's ongoing cosmic dance is filled with deep wisdom that will bring you back to your soul's messages and put you in tune with your personal truth. The Moon reveals your driving emotional needs and lights the path of healthy self-gratification. Understanding your own needs accelerates and enriches your emotional maturity. The more you know about your lunar energies, the more you will be able to develop and experience satisfying relationships with others. You can claim and communicate what it is you need to receive and to give in order to feel loved, heard, seen, and respected.

Below are descriptions of each of the twelve natal Moon signs, along with discussions of how they apply to healing potentially unconscious maternal connection energies that you may have been feeling and holding for your whole life. This may also include generational energies that were transferred to you from family members, from ancestors, or from your biological mother.

Moon in Aries (Fire, Cardinal, Masculine)

Dynamic, Energetic, Motivated, In Command

The Moon in Aries likes to go first! The driving need of this active Moon sign is to assert itself with confidence and to express itself in a way that builds independence and leadership. Those with a natal Moon in Aries seek to be inspired and

want to be #1 in everything they experience, making them competitive and fiery. When their energy is channeled toward something purposeful, it can be productive and help to accomplish a lot in a short time. If you are an Aries Moon, you need a way to move energy every day—through exercise or something physical that supports putting the desire for action into motion.

One of the main areas of learning for the Aries Moon is the opportunity to stay mindful of others and really hear and understand what other people need. As you mature, you gain awareness of how your actions may affect others. When you do have strong reactions and frustrations that flare up in anger, you will be presented with opportunities to harness this energy in other ways—for instance, through meditation or mindfulness practices that support hearing your quiet inner voice. Ultimately, you benefit from a daily regimen of self-improvement, which keeps your dynamic energy from hurtling toward others in combative or competitive ways.

- *Your Moon in Aries energies show up as*: strong initiative, independence, motivation, inspiration, impatience, fiery passions that burn out quickly, a desire to be first, a need for immediate gratification, a need to release energy, moving too fast for others, being childish, being unconsciously self-centered.

- *To balance these energies, learn to*: slow down and step back, think things through before acting, look at what you want objectively, consider how your actions will affect others, manage impulsiveness.

These qualities can reveal a dynamic relationship with your primary maternal figure. Are you a leader? Are you the first to do something in your family? Are you very independent? If so, your mother's reaction to your Aries lunar qualities will be influenced by her own Sun and Moon signs. You will interact differently with a Leo mother than you will with a Pisces mother. Whether or not you have a mother who is in tune with your own Moon's emotional needs, understanding how these unconscious maternal connection energies play out can help you heal any wounds or sore points for you in this area.

- *Your maternal connection energies may include*: excessive independence, relentless ego drive, being quick to anger, impatience, not feeling safe in yourself, feeling as if you need to fight for survival, a lack of tolerance for others, selfishness, narcissism, an inability to maintain healthy relationships.

- *To balance these energies, focus on*: calming down intense emotions, breathing deeply into the heart, feeling safe in your body, trusting yourself, developing better communication skills for problem-solving.

Moon in Taurus (Earth, Fixed, Feminine)
Grounded, Stable, Reliable, Strong

The Moon in Taurus is looking for what it can count on and tends to enjoy daily routines, familiar comforts, and set patterns. Those with this natal Moon hold a deep appreciation for the tactile world. They want to feel calm, to be surrounded by beauty, and to create peaceful experiences. They enjoy self-reliance, taking their own time, and observing before acting, which others may perceive as slowness.

If your natal Moon is in Taurus, you take financial matters seriously and work to create and maintain a strong sense of security. Monitoring how much money is in the bank, making careful investments, managing budgets, and assuring returns are all energies tied to the emotional needs of Taurus. As you mature, you have the potential to move away from overreliance on money, materialism, or possessiveness and generate a stronger sense of inner security that reinforces self-reliance.

No matter what happens in life, souls with the Moon in Taurus have the resources to handle unexpected developments by knowing that they have everything they need within themselves. When mature, they can draw on emotional supports that sustain them, so that they don't have to resist the changes of life.

- *Your Moon in Taurus energies show up as*: solidity, practicality, slowness, determination, reliability, a craving for stability, a desire for consistency, the enjoyment of beautiful experiences, a need for calming influences, a preference for knowing about change in advance in order to plan and prepare for it, a tendency to seek peace and calm, a need for grounding energies.

- *To balance these energies, learn to*: trust others to offer support, share what you own and what you value and think, recognize that you don't have to do everything on your own, trust that change can be good, understand feelings and deeper motivations.

These qualities can relate to the experiences you had of your mother when you were younger, as well as to generational patterns in your family around money, finances, and self-sufficiency.

- *Your maternal connection energies may include*: feeling unlovable or undervalued, needing to do everything on your own, fears around scarcity and making money, unhealthy financial relationships, sidelining your own creative spirit, feeling stuck or lazy, overemphasizing material status and possessions.

- *To balance these energies, focus on*: feeling solid and safe in your body, developing self-love mantras, trusting what feels meaningful for you, knowing that you are enough, transforming false beliefs about money and finances.

Moon in Gemini (Air, Mutable, Masculine)

Curious, Expressive, Communicator, Storyteller

Those with a natal Moon in Gemini have active, agile minds and a driving personal need to express themselves. This lunar energy wants to learn, to understand, and to gather more information, including gossip and the latest trending hashtags on social media. With experience and practice, Gemini energy develops principled communication, conversing and sharing responsibly and in line with its values. Gemini Moons may benefit from the daily private exercise of writing in a journal, speaking to themselves or into a voice recorder, or doing anything to express and release their thoughts. By moving their mental energy, they ward off spinning into anxiety. If you find yourself with too much going on and don't know what to focus on next, you may experience nervousness or restlessness or become overwhelmed.

Gemini Moons are fast learners and often very smart, with a strong desire to take in specifics, details, and information, and to keep learning. Sometimes they can spin complex, frenzied stories and narratives in their minds, leaving little momentum for follow-up actions.

The social, vivacious Moon in Gemini wants to interact with peers, schoolmates, classmates, siblings, and people on a daily basis. If this is your Moon, your natural affinity to connect and converse can drain your energy, however. Consider whether this is time well spent, or if are you spinning your wheels and not getting anything done. By following every trail of breadcrumbs or going down multiple rabbit holes without understanding what's really worth your energy, you may exhaust your active mind.

The growth opportunity for Gemini Moons lies in moving the energy from their heads into their hearts. It may take practice to drop into your heart space, but you will tap into a new energy source when you can access how you really feel and not just what you are thinking. Practice naming your feelings out loud, or write down what you feel as a way to harness your mental powers in service of emotional discovery and fortitude.

- *Your Moon in Gemini energies show up as*: intelligence, inquisitiveness, curiosity, a need to read or write or speak regularly, a tendency to seek out mental stimulation, a desire for daily movement and multitasking, flexibility and adaptability, inconsistency, flakiness, mental stress, anxiety, a risk of being "all talk and no action."

- *To balance these energies, learn to*: see the bigger picture, get out of your mind and feel more, trust yourself without needing exact details, temper mental stress or anxiety, feel your body and move emotional energy through it.

Your relationship with your mother may embody these qualities for you, as well. You may have experienced her as a strong communicator, an intellectual, a teacher, or a storyteller. If she wasn't those things for you, you may have sought out another maternal figure to tend to the need in yourself to validate your expressive nature. Gemini Moons may also absorb and hold anxiety from their mothers. You may have experienced her as disconnected to her emotional world, changeable, or restless.

- *Your maternal connection energies may include*: anxiety, feeling scattered, feeling as if you are not heard, feeling ungrounded, an overactive nervous system, a tendency to overthink everything, duplicity, leading a double life, trying to fit in, recklessness, never stopping to enjoy the simple things.

- *To balance these energies, focus on*: trusting your own voice, expressing yourself daily, meditating to calm your mind, developing mantras to avoid excessive thinking, grounding your daily energy.

Moon in Cancer (Water, Cardinal, Feminine)
Soft, Sensitive, Nurturing, Emotional

Those with the Moon in Cancer have a very open energy with a reigning desire to connect emotionally with others and have a safe place to share their hearts. The Moon is naturally at home in the sign of Cancer, which enables feelings to flow and energies to shift as emotions come and go.

Cancer Moons tend to have a rich internal experience. They are looking for emotional safety and security, as well as a sense of belonging. You may be tuned in to your inner world and the emotions that flow through it without much outward expression. For this reason, others may not be aware of what you're experiencing within.

Cancer Moons have a strong desire to build families, to feel safe in their home environments, and to create private places where they can retreat gently from communal life. From an early age, you may have learned to pick up on the energies in an environment, to sense what's going on around you. This may have been a survival strategy when you were younger when something in your family or home environment required you to internalize experiences and feelings.

As they mature, those with natal Moons in Cancer are invited to set aside defensiveness or the feeling of being too vulnerable. Stay open to the flows of life and the flows of your feelings as they move through for you. You're learning to take responsibility for how you feel and to know that you watch over your inner world. You are learning that you're equipped to support yourself. One of your strong emotional imprints is that you're here to mother yourself in this lifetime—to listen to your own feelings and needs and to give those to yourself, without blaming or expecting anyone else to provide them for you.

With your Moon in Cancer, you may have a hard time expressing how you feel to others. As you mature, you'll come to depend on the strength of your own emotions and open up to sharing how you feel with others in a healthy way. You do not have to keep your true feelings hidden, especially from people who love you, support you, cherish you, and want to know your heart.

- *Your Moon in Cancer energies show up as*: strong emotions, intuitiveness, a need to trust your own feelings, a desire to connect with others, a tendency to support loved ones, a need to create a safe place for others, nurturing energies, the ability to be a good listener, feelings of vulnerability, excessive sensitivity, a lack of awareness of your defensive tendencies, moodiness, a tendency to be unconsciously needy.

- *To balance these energies, learn to*: detach and not take things personally, be objective and grounded, step away from emotional reactions, manage high sensitivity, feel safe within yourself.

Your relationship with your mother from a young age formed your unconscious experiences of feeling safe. If your mother was nurturing, supportive, and present for you, you have moved through life trusting yourself and feeling secure. But if there was no one who connected with you emotionally, your experiences may have resulted in withdrawing and hiding your emotional needs to protect yourself and not feel vulnerable.

- *Your maternal connection energies may include*: not feeling safe, not feeling supported, not trusting emotional messages, excessive emotions, feeling scared of life, being overly defensive, feeling like a martyr to everyone's needs, being highly sensitive to other people, not feeling at home anywhere.

♦ *To balance these energies, focus on*: creating a safe and solid home for yourself, loving your vulnerabilities, developing tools to move through sensitive or emotional processes, trusting yourself and what feels correct for you, developing mantras for grounding.

Moon in Leo (Fire, Fixed, Masculine)

Confident, Creative, Proud, Bold

Leo Moons tend to be emotionally strong and expressive, with a reigning need to feel appreciated and respected. They are developing courageous hearts and learning to take risks to put themselves out there in the world. The healthy expression of the Moon in Leo is to share from a loving heart and to relish giving and receiving in equal measure. If this is your Moon, Leo's leadership energy guides your desire to do what you want, in your own way, even to the point of resisting other people's input. You can be very proud and stubborn, sometimes to excess.

As your Leo energy matures, you may uncover the ways in which you wore masks when you were younger in order to feel loved, to get attention, or to be seen. You learned how to perform in your search for emotional fulfillment from others. When you go deeper into what you truly need to feel validated, respected, and acknowledged, you will discover how you can feel naturally lovable without having to put on a show.

A Moon in Leo can also relate to having a strong mother in your life, whether her own personality is aligned with Leo energies or that's just how you experienced her. Perhaps your mother expressed that you were the leader of the family, that you were in charge. Perhaps she encouraged you to be creative and to embrace what you needed. Perhaps your mother was the first person who really saw you or who motivated you to be expressive and to understand your own talents.

Conversely, as a Leo Moon, you may have experienced the opposite. Perhaps you did not receive the attention or validation that you needed in your family or from your mother. In this case, you may have sought outside your family for ways to get your needs met. When you look at how Leo Moon energy has danced through your life, you can see how it either led to validation or showed up as the masks you needed to wear to feel loved.

- *Your Moon in Leo energies show up as*: creativity, strength, pride, confidence, a commanding and dominant personality, boldness, determination, unconscious self-involvement, a need for attention and for ongoing external approval, recklessness.

- *To balance these energies, learn to*: openly share without expectations, consider how your personal energy affects others, develop courage through conscious risk-taking, be okay without acknowledgment, trust your own creative process.

Leo Moons typically experienced their mothers as powerful figures who shaped them, whether or not they felt sufficiently safe or secure to express themselves openly. You may have experienced your mother as a very strong person who was in charge of the family and your life. You may have felt she supported your risk-taking and developing your confidence in yourself. Or you may have felt that you had to do certain things in order for her to see you and recognize you.

- *Your maternal connection energies may include*: not feeling powerful, not feeling seen, not feeling recognized, excessive attention-seeking, narcissism, making demands on others, controlling behavior, self-absorbed tendencies, an inability to give to others in healthy relationships.

◆ *To balance these energies, focus on*: feeling strong in yourself, developing your creative expression, owning your energy without needing validation, trusting your internal sense of self.

Moon in Virgo (Earth, Mutable, Feminine)
Efficient, Practical, Organized, Supportive

The Moon in Virgo has a driving need to organize, manage, and improve and to correct anything it deems wanting in its environment. Virgo is the energy of refinement, and this includes distilling your internal experiences. You focus in on exact issues and how they can be improved or healed. You tend to see your daily world through a practical lens and to establish routines around those priorities. Virgo is an Earth sign that approaches life through results-based decision-making. What can be sustained? What is necessary? What can I do on a daily basis to take care of myself? How am I going to show up to honor those needs and personal responsibilities?

Virgo Moons are strengthened through self-care, healing, understanding their bodies, working with their physical energy needs, and offering service and support to others. By maintaining a connection to your own needs and completing your daily routines, you gain a sense of order and well-being.

Virgo is where the mind meets the body, often resulting in strong mentalities that enjoy solving problems and helping others understand themselves. These Virgo insights bring novel perspectives to problems. You may find daily satisfaction in your work or in offering a specific skill set or expertise to others. As this energy matures, you're invited to implement the strengths you offer others on behalf of your own wants and needs. Get to the heart of what you need to feel healthy in all areas of your being.

This natal Moon can tend toward being too critical or too exacting, expecting perfection and precision when life can be messy. Allowing that things can unfold in multiple ways and that information doesn't always have to yield a certain picture can be useful to you. You can benefit from widening your focus beyond just what is wrong or what needs improvement. Accepting things as they are or learning to remain in a place of not knowing can both be powerful practices for Virgo energies.

The Moon in Virgo can find joy through satisfying work or daily habits. From the macro to the micro, from your purpose in the world to what you do every day, what you can do for others really brings about a feeling of satisfaction and usefulness.

◆ *Your Moon in Virgo energies show up as*: productivity, organization, a preference for routine, mindfulness, responsibility, dedication to you work, a desire for clarity and efficiency, helpfulness, the ability to apply knowledge skillfully, an unconscious martyr complex, feelings of inadequacy, feelings of guilt, perfectionism.

◆ *To balance these energies, learn to*: accept not knowing details, trust your intuition, be less hard on yourself, get out of your head, surrender control of a process.

You may have absorbed some of these messages in your experience of your mother. You may have felt that you needed to be a certain way—perfect, precise, following directions—in order to be loved. This may have been your first emotional imprint from your mother.

◆ *Your maternal connection energies may include*: perfectionism, not feeling seen, feelings of inadequacy, a guilt complex, a need to control relationships, excessive criticism, a martyr complex, a tendency to be at war with your body, ongoing health issues, feeling unconnected to a purpose.

- ◆ *To balance these energies, focus on*: listening to what your body needs, calming any critical internal messages, developing mantras for self-acceptance, knowing you are loved simply for being yourself.

Moon in Libra (Air, Cardinal, Masculine)

Connected, Chatty, Objective, Intimate, Sharing

Libra Moons have a driving need to relate to other people, to cooperate and share, and to talk about how they feel and what they're thinking. Working with and relating to others fulfills their natural gifts of understanding and sharing, of having conversations about feelings, and of being aware of the importance of speaking. Libra Moons gain greater clarity about what they are feeling by talking out their thoughts and emotions with someone else. This clarity may take you by surprise; you may be hit with a stroke of insight about what you need and feel or about your unconscious impressions of a person or situation.

This balanced Moon sign tends to stay steady and even-keeled on the emotional spectrum. Libras want time to process thoughts, to build a clear understanding of what they are feeling and what they need. But they can also get caught up in their own heads and not drop down into their hearts to really feel what is going on beneath the mind's activities. If your Moon falls in this Air sign, it will help you to go into a listening, receptive mode. It can be tricky to turn off your thoughts at first and step out of your comfort zone. But as you listen, you'll hear more of what's in your heart and perhaps learn more of what you need.

Libra Moons also need time alone to come back to themselves, and to hear what's really going on inside. They are learning to manage their own needs without projecting onto others. They can unconsciously expect others to fulfill their needs instead of taking personal responsibility and ownership.

If your Moon is in Libra, you are probably a people-pleaser. But you can float along unaware of all the effort you put into tending to other people's needs in order to sustain a relationship. You may struggle with putting yourself first. You may be hyperaware of other people and your environment, and you may be a keen observer of how to behave and what to say that will gain you respect. You may have an unconscious drive to be appreciated or to feel good by doing or saying what you think other people want to hear. You may try to preserve a conversation, a relationship, a friendship, or a connection by being "the good girl" or "the good guy."

Libra Moons tend to compare themselves to others. This energy of comparison, which can drive a back-and-forth internal conversation of which you remain unaware, can pull you away from what is essential for you. Over time, comparison can also weaken your sense of self-value and self-worth. Be careful not to place so much focus on others that you neglect strengthening your own sense of self.

The Moon in Libra excels at sharing with people and establishing relationships, but make sure you're also finding what you need in your relationship with yourself.

- *Your Moon in Libra energies show up as*: a tendency to be cooperative, great negotiating and diplomatic skills, objectivity, refined social skills, a desire for healthy relationships, a need to seek partnership and share opportunities, comparing and judging others, unconscious people-pleasing, a tendency to avoid conflict, codependency.

- *To balance these energies, learn to*: put your own needs first at times, feel strong being alone and developing your independence, handle disagreements on your own terms, avoid spinning in what others think, take action courageously.

Be aware of any messages around comparison and keep in mind that this could be an emotional imprint that you've been dealing with since childhood. This theme may have originated from your maternal relationship, especially if you felt your mother emphasized what other people might say or think about you or your family.

- *Your maternal connection energies may include*: codependency, comparison, not feeling loved, not feeling like an equal, excessive people-pleasing, allowing others to control or dominate you, not knowing your own needs, staying in situations out of fear of change or fear of being alone.

- *To balance these energies, focus on*: healthy communication techniques, being able to receive in all relationships, understanding what you need to feel loved by others, being independent in certain areas of life.

Moon in Scorpio (Water, Fixed, Feminine)
Passionate, Emotional, Transformational, Manifesting Alchemy

Scorpio Moons tend to have a very intense emotional world and bold desires. In fact, they often feel things at a deeper level than most and they often aren't aware of all the emotional intensity they experience, process, and manage regularly. They are here to master their powerful inner worlds as they dig into their internal messages and feelings. Because of these traits, they can be excellent counselors, therapists, healing guides, or psychologists who help others transform triggers and past traumas into new sources of personal power.

If your Moon is in Scorpio, you can also be highly attuned to other people's feelings. In fact, you may have felt intuitive or psychic your whole life. You see, feel, and sense things that not everyone perceives.

Scorpio Moons can be prone to emotional obsessions and emotional addictions, and not know how to manage them. But the journey of Scorpio energy is always about transformation. You are learning to take ownership of how you feel and to ensure that you are not absorbing feelings from others unecessarily. You may be holding energies for other people unconsciously, so it is important to establish clear boundaries around what is yours and what is not.

It may be enlightening to look at how these emotional power dynamics influenced you when you were younger. You may have absorbed emotional imprints from your mother or family members that deeply shaped whether or not you felt safe in the world. You may have experienced intense situations with other people when you were younger that were not healthy or loving. In fact, you may have encountered power games or control dynamics that made you feel powerless and were damaging to your individuality and self-sovereignty. If so, it's vital to your well-being that you embark on a healing path to empower yourself and own the truth of who you are and what you need.

If your Moon is in Scorpio, you need to have some type strategy for cleansing your emotions and your energy. This means that you need to move emotions through you so they don't get locked in or overly fixated on something or someone. You can bring your emotional vibration to a higher plane, rising out of those deeper, darker places. Enjoy your own mastery and revel in the fact that you are really capable of transitioning into a higher state of emotional expression. As you do this deep inner work, you can untangle from feelings that used to have a hold on you. You experience a new ability to trust yourself. You can learn to trust and love yourself fully.

Another part of your growth experience is learning to detach from your deep emotional experiences and to find a grounded balancing point. For example, you learn to see a situation with greater objectivity so that you're not always pulled into overwhelming feelings or intense reactions. Scorpio energy is here to master an emotional alchemy. You can work with the full spectrum of your inner world, from deep fears to passionate love, and feel powerful and balanced in how you do so.

- *Your Moon in Scorpio energies show up as*: passion, intuitiveness, intensity, strong emotions, a tendency to be probing, a tendency to be suspicious or domineering, a need to seek deeper understanding, obsessiveness, a desire for and enjoyment of intimacy, an unconscious need to control, power hunger, a need for emotional validation, an unknowing tendency to manipulate or spin, overattachment to others, jealousy.

- *To balance these energies, learn to*: step back and not be overly invested in relationships or situations, give people room and space, move past emotional responses to everything, develop your own healthy emotional process, monitor your mental spiraling.

You may have experienced your mother through these Scorpio themes, especially when you were very young and she was fully in charge of your world. You may not have felt safe or emotionally connected at times, and you may have been subjected to harsh power dynamics in relationships. You may have been raised in an environment where power and control deeply shaped you and your ongoing experiences of partnerships, friendships, and interactions with others.

- *Your maternal connection energies may include*: obsession, feeling unloved, early childhood trauma, any forms of abuse, intense emotional processes, emotional manipulation, power dynamics in relationships, domineering relationships, financial fears, unhealthy desires and addictions.

- *To balance these energies, focus on*: healing sacral chakra energies, developing healthy emotional processes, letting go as needed, balancing yourself with practical, grounded mantras.

Moon in Sagittarius (Fire, Mutable, Masculine)

Inspirational, Adventurous, Expansive, Restless

The Moon in Sagittarius brings positive, upbeat energy that looks for the next daily adventure. Those with this Fire sign have a reigning need to explore, learn, and grow, and experience the world around them to further understand what they believe. Sagittarius Moons yearn to engage in interesting conversations on a wide range of topics and to continue learning as a form of soul growth.

As a Sagittarius Moon, you feel things in a big way, from excitement around a potential trip to the disappointment of being let down by someone. When you feel a rising energy within, you're energized and ready to go. When the feeling passes or the energy shifts, you move on to the next experience and do not want to be bothered by the past. You value independence and the freedom to do what you want every day. You may choose to bring along people in your life whom you find emotionally fulfilling to share the adventure with you. But you can feel restless when you're bored or perceive yourself as trapped.

You may feel as if you're on a wild roller-coaster ride of feelings, overwhelmed one moment and then less interested once you've experienced the initial thrill. Your emotional mastery in this lifetime entails finding a healthy middle ground between the extremes. When you can stabilize your inner emotional turmoil a bit, you remember that you're ultimately in control of it. Then you can mine the gifts in both the highs and the lows.

Sagittarius Moons tend to seek out wide-ranging life experiences that shape how they view the world. Your array of knowledge gives you bold, assured opinions. You know what guides you—what you've learned, what you've experienced, what you believe, what is correct for you. And yet these understandings are for *you*. It is wise to stay aware of how these energies of righteousness—which can lead to being a know-it-all or thinking you have all the answers—may unconsciously be creating rifts in your relationships. You are mastering how to be strong in your own sense of self, while allowing room for others to hold different opinions and beliefs.

Sagittarius Moons are seeking to live an inspired life and want to keep learning. They are challenged to stay open to differences and other ways of moving through life. You may have had early childhood experiences that revolved around religion, opinions, belief systems, and spirituality. You may have grown up in a strict environment where you were told what to believe because it was "right" or "the best." This may have led you to be judgmental of other belief systems in the world. Thankfully, you enjoy exploring what supports you spiritually and what you believe in at different phases of growth. So you can accept and appreciate what is true for you now, even if it's different from what your family, your ancestors, or your community told you to believe.

- *Your Moon in Sagittarius energies show up as*: an adventurous nature, independence, wisdom, lifelong learning, positive attitudes, a great sense of humor, an ability to ride emotional waves, trust in your intuition, restlessness, inconsistency, unconsciously imposing expectations on others, being opinionated and judgmental, letting yourself be guided by belief systems.

- *To balance these energies, learn to*: ask questions and not make assumptions, stay open to other people's thoughts and opinions, monitor unconscious expectations, engage in reciprocal conversations, seek specifics and gather details.

You may have experienced your mother or maternal figure through these Sagittarian themes when you were younger, especially if she had strong beliefs, opinions, religious perspectives, or judgments about the world. You may have learned to be or act in a certain way in order to be accepted by her, or you may have been afraid of being alienated and judged for being different. Your mother may also have nurtured your adventurous nature and your expansiveness. She may have encouraged you to keep learning and exploring the world. If that couldn't happen in person in your young life, you may have pursued these goals through books, art, and performance.

- *Your maternal connection energies may include*: firm beliefs imposed in early childhood, a judgmental upbringing, a clear sense of right and wrong, a feeling of "us vs. them," feeling unseen, feeling undervalued, fear of being different, fear of being persecuted and judged, a tendency to follow the crowd.

- *To balance these energies, focus on*: openly accepting differences, exploring new belief systems, trusting intuitive messages, allowing waves of emotion to be part of the adventure.

Moon in Capricorn (Earth, Cardinal, Feminine)

Productive, Responsible, Mature, Committed

Capricorn Moons have a driving sense of responsibility that can show up as industriousness and being focused on their obligations. If your Moon is in Capricorn, you may feel or act more mature than others your age. You came into the world needing to take care of others, perhaps even literally taking care of family members or even your parents from a young age. You may have felt like an adult, even when you were a child. You may have been very focused on creating a stable life, and you were perhaps driven by a need to be respected. Every Moon sign wants to be respected, but Capricorn Moons really want to be taken seriously. They approach life asking what they can do each day that matters. If this is your natal Moon, your sense of purpose probably started early, whether you were an entrepreneur at eleven or started a movement or organization as a teenager or young adult. Your sense of who you are in the world remains tied to your everyday actions in pursuit of ambitious goals.

Capricorn Moons can be hard on themselves and believe that they are not doing enough. Their focus on productivity and achievement can also detach them from what makes them truly happy. Remember to experience joy in your life. It's not all about work or obligations or taking care of everything. You also have a responsibility to your own well-being, to your heart, and to your needs.

Be careful that your grounding in the physical world doesn't leave you unaware of how other people are feeling. You are learning to check in with your own emotional landscape and to make sure that your heart is energetically open. A strong connection to emotional energy may show up in other areas of your natal chart, in which case your Capricorn Moon may speak to a lack of nurturing emotional experience when you were younger. Maybe you didn't feel it was okay to be expressive or sensitive as a child. Maybe you just had to keep a straight face and tend to your chores. Or maybe you chose to stay focused on the work that needed to be done.

It may be helpful to look back on some of your own emotional programming. Are there emotional needs that your younger self didn't understand or acknowledge? How do these come up for you now? We all exist on an emotional spectrum and have parts of ourselves that need to feel loved, heard, and understood. The Moon in Capricorn may have shut down parts of your experience at a young age. But once you open up to them, you are able to tune in to more of your emotional expression and more of your strength.

◆ *Your Moon in Capricorn energies show up as*: dedication, responsibility, a serious nature, maturity, a preference for being in charge, a need to seek recognition, ambition, a focus on achievement, difficulty making emotional connections, a tendency to be intimidating or cold or domineering, an unconscious need to manage others, including family members and parents.

◆ *To balance these energies, learn to*: open up and feel your heart, allow others to support you in return, relinquish being in charge all the time, give yourself a break, focus on what makes you happy.

Capricorn Moons may have experienced these energies in their relationship to a mother or maternal figure. You may have experienced your own mother as distant, unavailable, or emotionally detached or perhaps as the hardworking person who kept the family together and managed everything in the household. She may have been focused on doing her own work and getting things done, instead of asking how you were feeling or allowing herself to be nurtured when needed.

◆ *Your maternal connection energies may include*: a need to be responsible for everyone, a tendency to manage family affairs, a desire to control others, feelings of being more mature than your siblings, feeling unrecognized, feeling as if you had no childhood, a need to work or be productive, an excessive fear of failure, an inability to relax or experience happiness.

◆ *To balance these energies, focus on*: stepping back from excessive doing for others, tapping into your feelings, allowing others to support you, developing a joyful activity or hobby.

Moon in Aquarius (Air, Fixed, Masculine)

Dynamic, Rebellious, Creative, Visionary

Aquarian Moons have a driving need to be unique individuals in the world and to contribute something special to others. This is the energy of wanting to do something different, working to make a difference, and seeing things from new angles. Aquarian Moons are often ahead of the curve and want to use their mental creativity in some way that gratifies them. This Moon encourages you to be an individual, to reject blending in with the crowd, and to discard the idea that you have to belong to something bigger than yourself. You may tend to find your relationships outside of your immediate family, and your first sense of feeling connected to others may derive from a group of friends, or perhaps one good friend who really sees you as you are.

As Aquarian Moons mature, they want to be with individuals who are as strong in their own self-images as they are. With these people, they can enjoy expressive, accepting conversations about what they feel and their sense of themselves in the world.

If your Moon is in Aquarius, you may be misunderstood or perceived as quirky at first, especially when you are younger. But this is usually just a response to your unique ways of doing things. You may go left when others go right or need more space or independence to do things your own way. With your Moon in an Air sign, your thought processes are paramount, and you'll want to cultivate some ways to move all those thoughts out into the world in a consistent way. Just as with other Air signs, you can best hear yourself think when you express your thoughts. So talking, speaking, writing, and getting it all out of your mind will always be important for you. As you release the pressure of your mind, you can start to open up to more of what you need and how you feel in your heart.

If this is your natal Moon, you may have had a very unusual childhood. Maybe there was something very different about your mother, your family, or your immediate environment that made you feel as if you were ostracized or set apart from the collective. You may have gained strength, however, because of that type of upbringing.

The Moon in Aquarius is here to contribute to the future. You are tuned in to forward-looking thoughts and inspiring life questions. What is possible next? Where are we going? What inspires me every day? What is my vision of my life? When you tap into those parts of yourself, you clarify what you're creating in your immediate daily surroundings.

♦ *Your Moon in Aquarius energies show up as*: rebelliousness, independence, creativity, a quirky and unique personality, a desire to be a trendsetter, a thirst for knowledge, an overactive mind, a desire to contribute to humanity, detachment from emotional expression, feeling out of place, uncertainty about your gifts, a yearning for belonging and connection, an excessive need to be around people, hesitancy to be independent.

♦ *To balance these energies, learn to*: feel peaceful without other people, be strong in your sense of self, trust your gut and intuition, go your own way as needed, accept recognition and acknowledgment.

Your mother or maternal figure may have represented these Aquarian themes in your life as a child, especially if you were rebellious, quirky, independent, or different in some way from your friends. You may have felt as if you were ostracized, abnormal, or a misfit, or that you didn't belong, even in your immediate family.

♦ *Your maternal connection energies may include*: feeling unaccepted or like an outcast, feeling undervalued, feeling as if you were denied independence, a tendency to be overly rebellious, inconsistency and unreliability, alienation, not feeling at home anywhere, feeling disconnected from your own power, an inability to listen to other people's views or thoughts.

- *To balance these energies, focus on*: being receptive to various perspectives, developing a fulfilling connection to others, trusting what feels true for you, committing to meaningful consistency.

Moon in Pisces (Water, Mutable, Feminine)
Intuitive, Artistic, Sensitive, Private

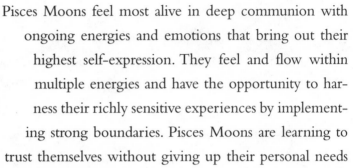

Pisces Moons feel most alive in deep communion with ongoing energies and emotions that bring out their highest self-expression. They feel and flow within multiple energies and have the opportunity to harness their richly sensitive experiences by implementing strong boundaries. Pisces Moons are learning to trust themselves without giving up their personal needs or self-identity to please others. They are developing an ability to be grounded in the real world, while also traveling to other planes of consciousness and spirit that allow them to be more open and free. Freedom is a keyword for this lunar type, as they desire movement and seek connection to an energy force bigger than their human selves.

Pisces tunes you in to the energies of your immediate environment, but also to those of a world beyond your immediate consciousness. You pick up a lot of emotions that are not yours. You may even feel weighed down by them. You may be made heavy by what you absorb at times, and not be certain where the influences are coming from. Pisces can help you practice intuitive mastery so you can trust what you feel. You can pick up on an understanding and allow that to be enough for you. It doesn't have to be processed or accepted through your mind; it's just how you feel. Trusting these intuitive messages can yield big rewards, as they open you up to new insights into your creativity or artistic expression or reveal an avenue of spiritual growth and development. All of this is part of your power.

Pisces Moons are private and need time alone to ride waves of melancholy or disconnection or feelings of powerlessness. Surrendering to the emotional experience that runs through you can take you far on the path to mastery as long as you don't overidentify with it. You are here to move through emotions as you continue to trust yourself.

You may have had a very intuitive experience with your immediate family, especially your main mother figure. You may have seen things or sensed things when you were younger that others did not perceive. It may be that one of your family members "disappeared" or that you felt abandoned by them in some way when you were younger. Pisces energy can show up as someone who wasn't there for you physically or emotionally no matter what the reason. And this may have triggered a sense of discouragement or a feeling of victimhood in you that started early on. Yet these deep emotional experiences formed an important part of your spiritual growth. As a Pisces Moon, you are here to connect to spiritual guidance, to go higher in your self-understanding, and to practice compassion and forgiveness. Experiencing loss and forgiveness in this way may be big themes in your life, especially with regard to your family members.

As you mature, you see the gifts of your intuitive messages and learn to trust yourself. You gain confidence in your own inner perceptions and become more skilled at interpreting them. Working with these gifts every day brings you ever more insight.

◆ *Your Moon in Pisces energies show up as:* an artistic nature, inspiration, a tendency to be psychic or ungrounded or isolated, creative gifts and a strong imagination that seeks expression, an ability to trust your emotional energies, unconscious escapism, victim consciousness, a tendency to blame others for needs that are not met, inconsistency, unreliability, a feeling of being overwhelmed by life.

- *To balance these energies, learn to*: be grounded and feel safe, honor responsibilities and routines, trust a purpose and direction, monitor self-pity or blame, avoid victim consciousness, focus on small details that make a difference.

You may have felt abandoned or ignored if your mother was not tuned in to your sensitivities and emotional needs. You may have found yourself sacrificing your own needs in order to be seen and loved by others.

- *Your maternal connection energies may include*: not feeling seen, a disappearing mother or father, addictions, abandonment, rejection, not feeling solid or grounded in your homelife, feeling highly sensitive, not being understood, wanting to be invisible, lacking willpower or self-assertion, lacking boundaries with others.

- *To balance these energies, focus on*: trusting and feeling your body, developing a spiritual perspective for your life, flowing with waves of feelings and emotions, saying no to others and building firm boundaries.

PART THREE

Your Mercury Sign

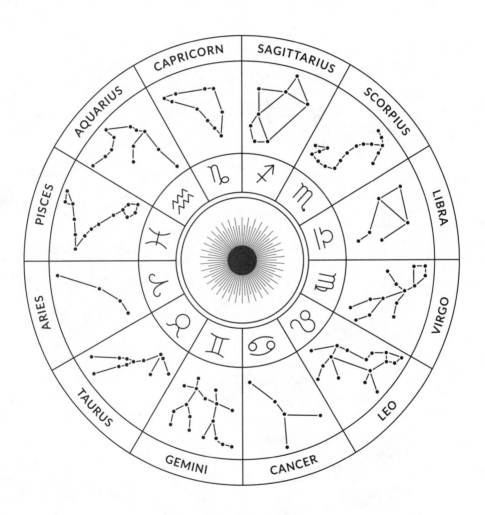

Chapter 5

Mental Energies

While your Moon sign speaks to your emotional world and daily needs, your natal Mercury connects to your mental capabilities and communication style. In Roman mythology, the god Mercury is the messenger and trickster. In astrology, we associate this god's namesake planet with how our minds function and perceive the world, including how we learn, communicate, and express ourselves verbally. Mercury also relates to everyday matters—to how we interact with our immediate environment, including electronics, communications, short-distance travel, and people like siblings, peers, and neighbors. As you connect with the energies of your Mercury sign, you may unveil interesting connections around how you learned new information at school or how you approach expressing your thoughts, opinions, and ideas. Your Mercury sign gives you what you need in order to understand new concepts and information fully and can provide insight into how you make decisions. All of these are in Mercury's domain.

We are never far from our thoughts and mental processes. In fact, for many people, the mind is the primary tool they use to move through life. Think of Mercury as your internal operating system, similar to the software a computer uses to manage all of the data and information it stores and processes. Mercury can help you upgrade this operating system by making you more conscious of how you understand and perceive the world around you as you take in all of the stimuli you encounter each day. Once you have a grasp of the basics of your Mercury sign, you will be better able to balance the energies in your mind and be more fully in charge of how you use your mental energy on a daily basis.

The Energy Spectrum

Each astrological sign contains a spectrum of energy that runs from its highest expression—your higher consciousness—to its lower expression—which you can think of as your lower consciousness. I tend to think of this range of energy as a set of musical octaves, with higher and lower vibrations. This harmonic relationship drives the dynamic pull between jealousy and passion, between flakiness and creativity, between obsession and attention. We move up and down this energy scale our whole lives; it's part of what makes us human. By becoming conscious of this spectrum and how you progress through it, you can balance your brain, increasing or decreasing the volume or pitch and enjoying the music you can make within.

Another way to visualize this process is to see energies opening and flowing between two signs on opposite, complementary sides of the astrological wheel. Just as when the two hemispheres of your brain hum along in harmony, you can move to new solutions and new perspectives. You can achieve a higher awareness and a deeper understanding of what is possible when your brain comes into balance. Much like the balance required to ride a bike, this mental balance manifests as an active state of constant discovery and adjustment.

Mercury Retrograde

You may have heard ominous warnings about Mercury retrograde, including advice not to buy electronics or sign contracts during these periods, which happen four times a year. When a planet is "retrograde," it simply means that, from our perspective on Earth, it seems to be moving backward in the sky. Mercury retrograde can be a time of mishaps, yes; but it can also open up a window in which we can reconnect, slow down, and access deep wisdom.

If you have Mercury retrograde in your natal chart, you probably need to sit and consider information more and allow yourself time before making decisions or communicating. For example, when a friend shares an opinion with you or gives you new information of some kind, you may just need to take it in and consider it before acting. The message of any retrograde planet—but especially tricky, impulsive Mercury—is all about harnessing energy internally first, before you blurt it out.

Harmony of the Spheres

There is an innate harmony in the zodiac that comes alive when opposite astrological signs work together. Think of the dynamic pull between opposing energies that we talked about above. You may already have these opposing energies in your chart thanks to the natal aspects of your five personal planets. If you have Mercury in Cancer and the Moon in Capricorn, for instance, your natal Moon will probably already be integrating the higher octaves of Capricorn themes into the harmonics of your natal Mercury.

This kind of harmony also shows up through the signs' elements: Water signs (Cancer, Scorpio, Pisces) work harmoniously with Earth signs (Taurus, Virgo, Capricorn); Air signs (Gemini, Libra, Aquarius) resonate with Fire signs (Aries, Leo, Sagittarius). This is true for separate individuals with harmonious charts, as well as for the relational aspects within your own chart. Even if you don't have very much of this balancing energy in your natal chart, however, you can still cultivate this harmony in a conscious way by drawing on the energies of these opposing signs. Any planet in a Water sign can work in harmony with its opposing Earth sign; every Air sign can resonate with the energies of its opposing Fire sign.

How does this work? Earth signs help define and offer clarity about what the Water signs are feeling, sensing, and processing. Just as the banks of a river provide definition and stability to the water's flow, Earth provides a practical approach to the emotional flow of Water. The reverse is also true. If you have Mercury in an Earth sign, the opposing Water sign supports it by letting things move and progress. By understanding these harmonic relationships, you can learn to allow movement and trust in a process so that things can move ahead even when you can't see them.

Likewise, the Fire signs (Aries, Leo, Sagittarius) are always opposed by Air signs (Gemini, Libra, Aquarius), which support talking through ideas, sharing what's on your mind, and being clearer on the specifics before taking action. Air signs are energized by Fire signs, which take those ideas and put them into action. The Fire signs inspire your next steps and ensure that you're actually *doing* something with all those thoughts running through your mind.

The harmony between the elements orchestrates a balance that is ultimately supportive. By actively working with your natal Mercury sign, you can begin to focus on what you are ready to develop next through the strengths of its opposing astrological sign.

Chapter 6

The Twelve Mercury Signs

In the following pages, you will find ways to harmonize the energies of your natal Mercury sign with the other energies in your chart and gain a higher perspective on its opposing astrological sign. If your natal Mercury is in Cancer, for example, its opposing sign is Capricorn. By understanding how the higher octaves of Capricorn can support your Mercury in Cancer, you can achieve a better balance when you're feeling pressured, stressed, or lost. This can be particularly beneficial as you learn to work with the lower octaves of your Mercury sign. For example, when you hit a mental block, or your monkey mind gets spinning, this balancing information can help you understand another perspective. Meditating on or working with this energy in your mind and your body can pull you out of your normal tendencies so you can move through mental stress and anxiety, resist being overwhelmed, and find greater objectivity and calm.

Mercury in Aries (Fire, Cardinal, Masculine)

Initiator, Motivational, Quick Thinker

Mercury in Aries is a dynamic, inspired communicator who often wants information, solutions, and plans *now*. If this is your natal Mercury sign, you may be known as a fast talker who urges things to move along quickly, and you may anticipate and expect rapid results, feedback, and progress. You may have

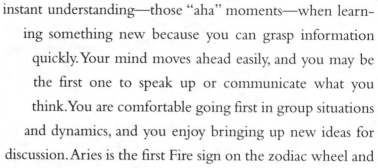

instant understanding—those "aha" moments—when learning something new because you can grasp information quickly. Your mind moves ahead easily, and you may be the first one to speak up or communicate what you think. You are comfortable going first in group situations and dynamics, and you enjoy bringing up new ideas for discussion. Aries is the first Fire sign on the zodiac wheel and is a natural initiator, which can come across in your communication style.

Those with Mercury in Aries can also be very focused on themselves. How does this affect me? How is this good for me? What do I want, and how can I get it? When your having a bad day, you may feel stressed-out, pouty, explosive, angry, frustrated, impatient, or impulsive. When your Aries mental chatter is trapped in these lower octaves, you have the opportunity to stretch your mind into the higher expressions of Aries' opposing sign—Libra. Libra energy is about taking a step back and getting out of your own limited world. It helps you to expand beyond your own process and subjective thoughts to see other possibilities. Libra reminds you to practice objectivity. Look at other people's needs, what someone else may be thinking or needing in the situation.

If your natal Mercury is in Aries, you may also be an unconscious self-involved talker who doesn't listen to or engage with others in a conversation. This may not be intentional, but when you see it in yourself, it can be beneficial to have a conversation with a friend to help you get out of your own head. You can also ask others you trust to tell you when they see this pattern playing out in you. Tap into the Libra energy of sharing and conversing. Libra offers you another way to look at things, and reminds you that not everything is about you.

If you're feeling angry, trace your feelings to the root cause. Perhaps allow situations to play out. Give them time and be willing to talk them out. One of the gifts of the Air signs is that they want to listen and discuss almost anything, which can be very beneficial for Mercury in Aries, especially when you want an answer or outcome *now*. Libra can help you establish a realistic timeline by pointing out that, although something may not happen today, it could still happen in a month or next year. This objective perspective can encourage you to balance your impatient impulses.

Another danger for you as a Mercury in Aries is that you can speak too fast and regret it later. The higher octave of Libra reminds you to give yourself breathing room before speaking so that your words don't come across as too intense or too rash. Words spoken impulsively can be sharp and harmful, which is probably not your intention. Mercury in Aries is learning how to allow time for solutions, to make some space, and to pull back to a wider perspective. The higher consciousness of Libra supports you as you learn to trust how a process can unfold, especially if you need help from others.

♦ *Mercury in Aries awakens through*: gaining perspective, taking extra time, trusting the process, asking for help.

Mercury in Taurus (Earth, Fixed, Feminine)
Self-reliant, Determined, Practical

Mercury in Taurus is very focused on what is seen and what is happening in the physical world—on the reality of life's current circumstances. Taurus is the first Earth sign on the zodiac wheel and has a driving desire to be self-reliant. Taurus energy does well on its own, especially when there is a reliable plan for how you want to move about your day. You can have an amazing determination to stick to an outcome and see something important through to completion. But those with Mercury in Taurus can also be very hard on themselves when they can't figure something out. They can get frustrated and stuck in a kind of mental heaviness—for instance, when trying to verify what is the right next step or best solution to a problem. They have a driving need for security, and their mental process really does need to find answers so that they can move forward. Every Earth sign is gifted with understanding the practical realities of their world, which can also bring up stress around money, finances, work, parenting, and life's responsibilities.

Mercury in Taurus is known for being an observer, perhaps from a distance, and taking in information that can be verified. The weight of the world can weigh on the Taurus brain, however, especially in terms of figuring out financial problems, not wanting to take big risks, or not wanting to move too fast on something until more facts are known. Pressure to solve something on your own can amplify this mental stress. No one is an island. But sometimes the Taurus mind can make you feel stranded as you try to figure out a conundrum or find clear results and tangible evidence to support your next steps.

If Taurus energy can strand you on an island of practical concerns, then we can see the water surrounding that island as the energy of Scorpio, which is Taurus' opposing sign on the zodiac wheel. The Water signs, especially Scorpio, reveal what's deep beneath the surface. Water invites you to tap into how you really feel and to trust these parts of yourself. The higher octave of Scorpio energy brings forward the transformational ability to trust what you can't yet see. Taurus energy needs to take a step back from its earthly reality at times and go into its feelings. When you do, you gain a better understanding of what is unconsciously driving your fears. Where does this stem from? When have I felt this before? What if I accept that I may never understand this—that I just have to feel my way through? Remember, Taurus is grounded in the earthly realms, while Scorpio water runs beneath the Earth's surface in underground caves, rivers, and springs. Go into these deeper parts of yourself and learn to feel more of what is driving your need for security. Know that flow exists even beneath impenetrable rock. You just need to ask yourself: What is this fear and how can I transform it through greater trust in myself?

Another strength you can gain from Scorpio energy is the ability to share your inner world with people you trust. Whenever there is too much on your Taurus mind, it can feel good to open up to a trusted individual and talk situations through in a way that releases your unconscious fears, limitations, or survival mechanisms. The higher octaves of Scorpio can then bring in additional perspectives, other resources, different support strategies, and better ways to move through a worry or a stress so you don't feel so alone or stuck.

- ◆ *Mercury in Taurus awakens through*: uncovering the root of a fear, letting emotions flow, sharing your inner world, opening up to trustworthy people.

Mercury in Gemini (Air, Mutable, Masculine)

Multitasker, Detail-driven, Curious

Mercury in Gemini is known for having a very busy mind that seeks stimulation, new information, social-media memes, and something fascinating to contemplate. Gemini is the first Air sign on the zodiac wheel and associated with our ability to communicate, learn, and speak about ourselves. Geminis are strong multitaskers with a lot of energy for ideas, projects, conversations, data, details, and understanding specifics. If this is your natal Mercury sign, you can live in your mind a lot, spinning in a variety of scenarios and details. All of this intense mental energy, however, can also create anxiety, feelings of being overwhelmed, an inability to focus, and a restlessness that can be tricky to harness. You may be juggling a lot of plates, and you may be worried that they may all come crashing down.

Sagittarius is the planet in opposition to Gemini, and the higher octaves of Sagittarius energy support you in taking a higher viewpoint of your priorities. Sagittarius allows you to see things with the eye of a hawk, from high above.

Disentangle from your mental process and look at where you're going. Consider what matters in the long term and discover what is really important beyond the narrow scope of what is in front of you at this moment. Understanding the landscape from high above lets you zero in on priorities for today. You don't have to feel scattered or overwhelmed by everything that needs to get done. Instead, take some deep breaths and look at what counts in the bigger scheme of your life.

If your natal Mercury is in Gemini, you want to have a destination for your thought processes, and Sagittarius can provide context and meaningful goals. Sagittarius helps you step out of your monkey mind and move your body, releasing any surplus energy or information. Let the basics of movement and fresh air shift your mental energy out of the spiral you may find yourself in. Let them slow your rapid thoughts to a more human pace that mirrors your own footfalls. No matter how far ahead your mind travels, your journey can only be undertaken step-by-step. The more you can practice calming your mind through movement, the more you will be able to prioritize what is in front of you right now.

It can also be important for those with Mercury in Gemini to talk or write out what's on their minds. Automatic writing, or stream of consciousness, can get all those thoughts out of your head so that you can look at them more closely and respond energetically to what's on the page. Notice what you feel as you express yourself, because that's also a gift of Sagittarius. Sagittarius will say: Yes let's go for it; I want to do it; that's right for me; that is correct for me. Instead of looking at all the tasks in front of you and thinking that you have to do them all, assess what is energetically correct for you through physical movement—talking or writing out your thoughts—and tune in to your energy field for more guidance. Then you can sense when you are genuinely excited about something you've been thinking about and how you can use that understanding to determine where you will focus next.

- *Mercury in Gemini awakens through*: thinking while you move, getting a bird's-eye view of a problem or situation, talking or writing out your thoughts, asking for others' opinions and ideas.

Mercury in Cancer (Water, Cardinal, Feminine)
Sensitive, Self-reflective, Emotional

Mercury in Cancer is gifted with speaking, sensing, and communicating information of a feeling nature through an intuitive lens. You tap into what's being said and how it is relayed, and you know how it makes you feel. Communication often inspires a strong response or feeling to rise up in you. At times, you can feel moody, emotional, defensive, or exhausted from what you're picking up in your environment. If your Mercury is in Cancer, you may often want time to process and be in your own world to think about what you're going to say, how you should say it, or what feels right. Your mind spends a lot of time and energy processing what you're feeling and how to discuss it. You may even feel hesitant to share what you need, since you have a sense of what others are feeling and you tend to anticipate their response. The sensitive Cancer energy wants to feel safe when it opens up to others, and you may need to practice building safe spaces and then trusting that you can let your thoughts, opinions, and needs flow.

Cancer's opposing sign of Capricorn can assist you by providing clarity, purpose, and a practical approach to communication. Capricorn energy asks you to take emotion out of the picture. Step back and look at the concrete facts, the details that matter, and the overall objective that you want to reach. When you risk spiraling into your feelings, the higher octave of Capricorn connects you with how something serves you. Is this meant for me right now? If so, go ahead and make a plan of action.

Capricorn supports expressing yourself in a strong, clear, and firm way. A forthright plan will help you move beyond your tendency to feel differently about things from day to day. On some days you may want to do something because it feels right, while on other days you may not want to do it at all because your energy has shifted. You are tuned in to the emotional energy of the moment, the day, and the week, riding the ups and downs as they come your way. Capricorn energy can help to ground you and give you an overarching understanding of your priorities so you can map out a reliable plan. Capricorn gives you strength, a backbone, a sense of purpose. It can remind you that your own strength can remain constant, regardless of the ebb and flow of the present moment.

The higher octaves of Capricorn support you by balancing out the highs and lows of your emotional tides. Allow Capricorn to guide you to a clearer objective for the long term and to sustain you on those off days when you don't want to get anything done. In this way, your Cancer soul can move through your process without giving up on your goals or your own needs.

- ◆ *Mercury in Cancer awakens through*: making a plan as needed, clarifying your goals, asking what serves you, practicing detachment and objectivity.

Mercury in Leo (Fire, Fixed, Masculine)

Expressive, Bold, Charismatic

Mercury in Leo exudes charisma, strength, leadership, and creativity. It is a Fire sign, which supports self-expression and encourages you to be bold and empowering when you share what you're thinking and understanding in a way that inspires others. You may enjoy public speaking and any form of communication that allows you to demonstrate your expertise in some manner.

Leo is a fixed sign. In its lower octaves, it can help your mind to be very focused on what you want and how you perceive things. But you may unconsciously become stuck on wanting things your own way, with no input from others. Those with Mercury in Leo can be unconsciously selfish or self-involved—unaware of how they come across to others and how their thoughts or ideas may be interpreted.

The sign opposite to Leo on the zodiac wheel is Aquarius, which is an Air sign that can connect you to the energy of the group or the collective. If your natal Mercury is in Leo, you can benefit greatly from discussing ideas with others and gathering feedback. This process fuels your creative fire and lights up new inspirations. Aquarius wants to help you see a higher way of doing things and encourages you to anticipate the road ahead so you can create for the long term.

The higher octaves of Aquarius will also help you understand how your communication style affects others, supporting your capacity to further develop leadership skills and public-speaking abilities. Aquarius feedback reminds you to be responsible with your words, clear in your meaning, and intentional about what you're putting out there so that you're received by an audience in the way that you want to be. You want to be recognized and noticed. You enjoy center stage, but may find it even more rewarding to know how you are coming across and that you are really landing your message. The higher vantage point of Aquarius can pull the blinders off of your ego and build your self-knowledge from a detached perspective. Consider the various viewpoints and interpretations that come from a variety of people. Are you being too rigid in your expectations and thinking process? Stay aware so that the tone of your delivery supports the content of your message.

Ultimately, the Aquarius energy coming back to Mercury in Leo can make you even more confident and proud, and clearer in what you need to say. In this way, you put your talents in service of something bigger than yourself.

♦ *Mercury in Leo awakens through*: processing and planning with others, gathering feedback from a group, checking your tone while speaking, considering how your information is being received.

Mercury in Virgo (Earth, Mutable, Feminine)
Self-critical, Process-oriented, Perfectionist

If your natal Mercury is in Virgo, you are a whiz at solving problems and a gifted observer—right down to the inner workings and the smallest minutiae. You get a bead on what's happening and assess what needs to be changed, improved, or healed. You are very good with puzzles, including working the pieces of the endless puzzles of everyday life to create the most efficient outcome or result. You are driven to seek perfection and resolution, but there are times when you can feel as if your efforts are not good enough. Guilt can set in and you can be hard on yourself. Why haven't I solved this? Why haven't I figured this out? Why isn't this running better? What else am I missing? Because you can and will see everything that is wrong or not working, you can become picky and critical. Without any bad intentions, your eye can catch faults and opportunities by second nature. But focusing on the problems, messes, and mistakes can make you difficult company for yourself and others.

Pisces lies opposite to Virgo on the zodiac wheel. This energy offers you the ability to step back, to zoom out from the details and minutiae, and to consider how the information you offer up makes people *feel*. Your analytical bent isn't going anywhere, so why not train your eagle eye on more nebulous targets, like how other people are interpreting what you are saying? Pisces energy helps build your "compassion muscle," especially when you're being hard on yourself or feeling a strong need for a particular outcome. Pisces reminds you to be gentle with yourself and to allow some of your worries to dissolve. You don't have to solve every problem, nor do you have to fix everything. Pisces relaxes you and allows you to accept the flow of life. Virgo loves the detailed process, but Pisces reminds you that, even when there's no process at all, things are still going to turn out perfectly. Acorns don't follow a blueprint as they grow into oak trees.

Pisces energy brings in acceptance, compassion, and a light touch for Mercury in Virgo's relentless drive toward improvement. Pisces can balance you energetically and relieve you of the need you feel at times for perfection or precision—especially if you have been carrying any martyr energy or if you've been self-sacrificing too much. Pisces can also help you take care of yourself. You can't improve the whole world, nor can you do everything for everyone. But perhaps you can be kinder to yourself today and allow that to be perfect enough.

◆ *Mercury in Virgo awakens through*: being kind to yourself, accepting the flow of life, finding perfection in what is, practicing letting go and trusting.

Mercury in Libra (Air, Cardinal, Masculine)

Gifted Speaker, Collaborator, Good Listener

Mercury in Libra brings the energy of connecting with people through conversation, sharing, and collaboration. If this is your natal Mercury, you are a gifted speaker and communicator, often knowing the best way to make your points and demonstrate your perspective. You excel at listening and discussing matters of all kinds, including topics that may initially be difficult or create conflict. You can weed out what's important and what's needed from a swamp of conflicting viewpoints and reactions. You are very intelligent and can process a lot of information from other people and outside sources. You genuinely seek to understand others' points of view.

Mercury is very strong in Libra. You are naturally focused on the other partner or parties involved in any given situation, and you have a gift for finding harmony. You are a natural conversationalist and can probably talk with anyone about almost anything—with charm. Your Mercurial energy wants to solve problems, work cooperatively, and summarize what is needed to complete projects or plans. You are probably the go-to person when problems arise, as well as a good listener when someone needs advice. You exude many strengths that people appreciate and value.

However, the lower octaves of Mercury in Libra may find you biting your tongue to keep the peace, or people-pleasing, or saying what you know others want to hear instead of what they need to hear. You may hold back or betray your values when you really should speak out. But Aries, opposite to Libra on the zodiac wheel, brings a self-assured energy that reminds you to show up as yourself without compromise. You need this strong backbone to avoid getting caught in endless cycles of deliberation and consensus-building. Have you ever fallen prey to analysis paralysis? Maybe you just want to keep a conversation going, perhaps out of fear of hurting someone's feelings or of coming on too strong. Mercury in Libra wants to be liked and accepted, and to engineer win-win scenarios. If you feel that someone doesn't agree with you, you can consciously draw on the higher-octave energy of Aries, which reminds you of your authentic individuality. Not to worry—the right people will connect with you based on who you truly are.

People-pleasing or making excessive comparisons can tank your energy. The balancing influence of Aries reminds you that it's courageous to be who you are. It's okay to put yourself first at times and get clear on what you need. You can include yourself and make yourself a priority as well.

The balancing energy of Aries can also help you to trust yourself to make good decisions. It can allow you to turn off your head and trust the messages in your body—your gut feelings and your physical energy levels—because Aries rules physical vitality. Notice your body's messages in the form of sensations: rising energy, gut feelings, vibrations or tingling, flushed excitement. Practice listening to these messages as a part of your decision-making process. They can direct you to your highest priorities and greatest good.

- ◆ *Mercury in Libra awakens through*: trusting your gut, prioritizing yourself, claiming your authentic self, listening to what you need and want.

Mercury in Scorpio (Water, Fixed, Feminine)
Intuitive, Passionate, Counselor

Mercury in Scorpio is often a very intuitive communicator who can uncover hidden energies and influences that other people miss. Those with Mercury in Scorpio may intensely feel what is happening beneath the surface, and they are unafraid of honesty. They are passionate, intense, and driven to understand more of what is going on, especially through research, deep inquiry, talking through sensitive matters, and getting to the heart of an issue. They willingly approach topics that others deem taboo or off-limits. But, in fact, these areas light up their curiosity to understand and know more.

This Mercurial energy seeks truth and wisdom through all facets of knowledge. You may be guided by passions for certain topics, hobbies, industries, or specialties. You are a detective capable of intense focus and unrelenting resourcefulness. You probably delight in connecting with people and making them feel safe to share their innermost wounds, fears, and desires. Those with this energy are often gifted therapists, counselors, healers, and guides who help others connect with their hidden truths or repressed stories.

Mercury in Scorpio in its lower octave can participate in power struggles and control dynamics. You may even fall into habitual patterns of ranking yourself and others according to your needs and wants. You may brace yourself for battles you think you'll have to fight. You can fall into envy and jealousy and imprison yourself in the misery of comparing yourself to others.

Whenever these expressions arise in your mind, you can balance them with the strength of Taurus. Taurus energy is grounded, clear, and aware of what works. Taurus knows what is necessary. When Mercury in Scorpio falls into a desperate passion—which can feel like too much for some—shifting into the higher octaves of Taurus can remind them of what is essential right now. Taurus energy can tether you to the present moment, pull you back into your physical reality, and ground your intense emotion with real-world support. One of the quickest ways to access Earth energy is to put your hands on a tree or some other plant, or just take off your shoes and put the soles of your feet in the grass or soil. You will feel clearer in your energy and your priorities will emerge from the haze of your emotional storm. Mercury in Scorpio needs clarity to be in this world and to connect with abundance—of the Earth, of natural resources, and of the simple joys in life itself.

Taurus takes care of what needs to be taken care of in order to access the energy of abundance associated with this sign. When you are overwhelmed by a maelstrom of anxiety, fear, or rage, Taurus energy will help get you centered in your body and in the world, and give you simple steps you can take. The simplicity of Taurus balances Scorpio's complexity. How can you take a big topic or issue and break it down into manageable pieces? What is the next smallest step you can take? What is the simplest explanation for a difficult situation? Use the Earth itself to ground and support you.

◆ *Mercury in Scorpio awakens through*: grounding into earth, feeling centered in the body, breaking things down into simple steps, turning your attention to a concrete result.

Mercury in Sagittarius (Fire, Mutable, Masculine)

Inquisitive, Inspirational, Mystic

Mercury in Sagittarius is a big thinker, a mystic, a seeker, and a dreamer. This individual's mind loves seeing the grand picture and unlimited potential and longs to understand, learn, and know more of what is happening in the world. Those with this natal Mercury have an inquisitive streak that explores new possibilities and pursues fascinating topics or ideologies. They gather a lot of wisdom, and then happily share it with others. They unspool interesting knowledge and facts gleaned from a lifetime of boundless curiosity. They may hold strong opinions about what is important and useful, as their Sagittarius energy prefers to make informed choices based on their own life experiences. They may adhere to passionate beliefs or philosophies about life.

If your natal Mercury is in Sagittarius, you prefer expansion, and may even communicate in a grandiose manner to make your point. But your forceful opinions on world issues and on what you believe is right or wrong can lead to unconscious judgments about what others should do or believe. The lower expressions of this Mercury sign may cause you to come across like a know-it-all, especially if you have studied, traveled, and investigated a lot in your life.

The balancing influence of Gemini, Sagittarius' opposite on the wheel, can support your Mercury thought processes by keeping you open and asking questions. It reminds you that you don't have all the information or all the answers. Gemini supports you by showing you that there's always more to understand.

How can I see this differently? What specific questions can I ask to gather more information? Can I hold two or more opposing truths at the same time? Inquisitive conversations, back-and-forth exchanges, and listening to those who are radically different from you will continue to open your eyes and pique your interest. Though it may not come naturally to you, you can learn to accept and validate multiple versions of the truth. Gemini energy allows you to have intellectual exchanges and to listen to more perspectives. Remember that everything is a story, and there are an unlimited number of stories in the Universe. Gemini energy tunes you in to the infinite number of viewpoints that coexist in the world. These perspectives can be endlessly fascinating and can spur your ongoing growth.

+ *Mercury in Sagittarius awakens through*: holding multiple truths at once, trying out other viewpoints, renewing your curiosity, remaining open to new details and pieces of information.

Mercury in Capricorn (Earth, Cardinal, Feminine)

Responsible, Conservative, Clever

Those with Mercury in Capricorn are clear communicators who often choose words carefully and understand the impact their comments will have. They are typically serious, and can come across as the strong-but-silent type. They may also be natural observers. This Mercury is often very business-minded, responsible, and focused on managing the job at hand. However, they are also known for being clever and having a well-timed sense of humor. The mental and conversational aspects of Mercury can be quite effective in Capricorn, and they can help you discern what needs to be said—and what is better left unsaid. Your mind is geared toward results and realistic outcomes in any area of life. But you are also focused on long-term planning and, for that reason, can feel more conservative at times. Any risks you take must be tied to a calculated and strategic long-term plan.

The lower octaves of Mercury in Capricorn can feel stoic, standoffish, or harsh. You may come across as condescending at times or give the impression that no one else is as qualified as you are. You may sometimes not want or need other people, so you may isolate yourself or appear to be unwilling to trust others or work with them. You enjoy being alone in your own thoughts, which can lead others to mistake your reserve and reticence as snobbery and secrecy.

The sign opposite Capricorn on the zodiac wheel is Cancer, which connects to your heart and how you feel. Cancer reminds you that you can fulfill your responsibilities and achieve your goals in a warmhearted manner. The balancing influence of Cancer will help you tap into what is correct for you and how it makes others feel, which you may not naturally consider. Though you are perceived as a leader and in control of things, there are times when you need support as well. Cancer energy will connect you with people who want to be on your team or partner with you. You don't have to do it all alone. Allow Cancer energy to connect you with others. This can open you up to new potentials and soften some of your rougher edges. Cancer energy offers you a respite and a chance to take a deep breath when facing day-to-day realities and whatever mountain you're climbing.

Mercury in Capricorn can feel hardened by the realities of life or focused on set values and destinations. Cancer energy wants you to know that it is okay to soften. Remember your own childlike innocence. What drew your spirit before you had to take on so much responsibility? In what ways were you soft before you had to be strong? It's okay to take a day off. Give yourself a vacation and some downtime. Take a deep breath and allow yourself to receive rather than always giving. Cancer energy can help you bring your daily habits into balance as you make yourself a priority.

- *Mercury in Capricorn awakens through*: seeking and accepting support, softening within your strength, receiving abundance, asking others how they feel about an idea or perspective.

Mercury in Aquarius (Air, Fixed, Masculine)

Complex Thinker, Forward-looking, Perceptive

People with Mercury in Aquarius are inquisitive thinkers with fascinating minds who understand complex concepts and intricate systems. Creative ideas move through their minds in a constant flow; they bounce through conversations, ideas, projects, and relationships. They live in an exciting world, always perceiving things anew and gaining more advanced ways of understanding the world. They have a clear idea of where they're going and what they want, so much so that they can become very fixated on what matters to them and how things should happen. If this is your Mercury sign, your search for new meaning and higher perspectives emboldens your big dreams and high ideals. You enjoy the gift of juggling many things at once, which brings with it the challenge of ensuring you are following what is correct for you and not just going along with the crowd.

As a fixed sign, Aquarius gives you a firm idea of what you want and how you expect it to happen. This can include a sense of underlying control, a reluctance to share, or a tendency to keep others at arm's length. You need your mental freedom and independence, so there are some parts of your life that you want to keep for yourself. Yet staying too much in your own world can lead to stagnation and disconnection from your original passion.

The opposing sign of Leo brings you back to what lights you up. It highlights what's most worthy of your energy in the bustling, harried marketplace of your mind. It helps you connect with your sense of self for answers without getting swept into the whirlwind of answers and influences outside of you. Where do you feel energized and excited within yourself?

Aquarius energy needs the fire of life, which pulls you out of your head and into your heart space. How do I feel about this? What do I want? Is this in alignment with my life's direction? The balancing influence of Leo will bring you back into your sense of power and self-expression. You're moving from focusing unconsciously on external energy and dropping down into your body for its golden messages. You will feel energized by the treasure you find there, and embrace the courage to be yourself even more in the world.

◆ *Mercury in Aquarius awakens through*: reconnecting with your heart's desire, easing up on control, homing in on one thing at a time, listening to what you truly want.

Mercury in Pisces (Water, Mutable, Feminine)

Sensitive, Empathetic, Self-expressive

Mercury in Pisces swims in intuitive, creative, and sensitive energy. You are an empath who picks up on what is unexpressed—what lies beneath the surface of everyday interactions. Your rich inner world senses a lot in the physical world and sees beyond the quotidian and into what is rare and magical. Your gift for creative self-expression allows you to share from the heart.

Those with Mercury in Pisces are known for being very good listeners and generous friends. Even when you are not sure of the exact words to use, you can communicate what you're feeling in a way that opens up people's hearts and brings them into your personal experience. You give good advice and offer helpful feedback, because you want people to see the best in themselves. You tend to gravitate toward spiritual understandings and deeper meanings of life. You can know exactly what to say in tough situations, especially when you trust your intuition and tap into what you feel others need.

Your artistic and creative gifts can sometimes feel thwarted and overwhelmed by the realities of life. The lower octaves of Pisces can sometimes make you feel overwhelmed, depressed, discouraged, and powerless. When you feel as if you don't know what to do, or you don't know what steps to take, you may end up shutting down before you can do anything. This Water energy can leave you feeling as if you're floating in the ocean without anything firm to hold on to, staring at an endless, infinite horizon. You need a higher perspective you can trust to keep from sinking. You benefit from having a spiritual understanding of and connection to the Universe, which serves as a North Star to guide your internal emotional process.

Virgo lies opposite to Pisces on the zodiac wheel. Virgo energies can give you discernment, practical advice, and reality checks. Their balancing influence reminds you of your daily responsibilities and encourages you to keep life simple—feed the dog, take a shower, get the mail, make lunch. Virgo energy grounds you and shows you what to focus on and what you can do to avoid being overwhelmed. It grounds the bigger feelings you have and offers you a way to manage those energies responsibly through a daily routine that attends to the details. When you feel as if you're in that open ocean, just floating around and not knowing what to do, Virgo throws you a lifeline that helps you make decisions. What are the pros and cons? What are the top three things that need to happen next? Just asking yourself these questions invites Virgo to help you come up with a process or a plan to follow.

- ◆ *Mercury in Pisces awakens through*: articulating your next smallest step, rising to a higher perspective, strengthening your daily routines, focusing on what is essential.

PART FOUR

Your Venus Sign

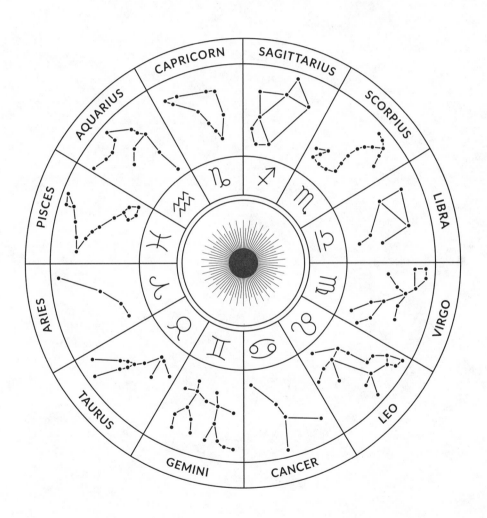

Chapter 7

Feminine Energies

Venus is like a tree with roots that extend deep into the earth and water, and branches that reach up into the air and warm sunlight. Venus speaks to your nourishment and receptivity, as well as to how you entwine with others, cooperate, isolate, and grow. What kind of tree would you be? Do you feel best standing alone in a field or enmeshed in a deep forest? Do you thrive on the banks of a river or in the high desert? Do you have dense, thick bark or willowy, loose branches? When you know these parts of yourself, you know your Venus energy.

Venus is the feminine energy of receiving, and also of how worthy you feel of receiving from others. Like the ancient goddess whose name she shares, Venus is associated with love, value, and self-worth. By extension, Venus is connected to finances, relationships, and friendships with women. Venus also dictates the tone and quality of your connections to others, and essentially how you relate to all energies around you. What do you need to feel loved and seen? What feeds your self-consciousness and expands your ability to experience pleasure? How do you relate in friendships, partnerships, and relationships of all kinds?

Whether you're accepting a small compliment or a big gift, whether you are receiving someone else's love and affection, whether you feel worthy of being valued, cared for, and adored—Venus energies move through all these and more.

At its deepest level, Venus energy is rooted in what you believe about your own worth and how you love yourself. How do you receive?

The Divine Feminine

The Divine Feminine embodies higher consciousness, responsible relationships, strong personal values, and authentic openheartedness. Your natal Venus sign—the sign Venus was in at the time of your birth—can help you evolve into a fuller expression of these qualities by awakening the Divine Feminine energies associated with each astrological sign. Your natal Venus expresses these energies within you, revealing how you love and accept yourself at a core level. Harmonizing with your Venus sign raises your consciousness around love, sharing, receiving, connecting, and feeling more confident in your own skin.

Divine Feminine energies tend to awaken deeper truths that may have been blocked or suppressed earlier in your life. They can help people of all genders feel drawn to being softer, more receptive, and more open to sharing their feelings. These expressions will be unique to you. As you awaken to and receive more love within your energy field, you may start to feel subtle shifts. You may yearn for deeper, truer connections—starting with your relationship to yourself. Reconnecting with these Divine Feminine energies will elevate your sense of self-worth and create new potentials as you honor more of your own essential worthiness.

Venus Retrograde

As discussed in chapter 5, when a planet is "retrograde," it simply means that, from our perspective on Earth, it seems to be moving backward in the sky. If you have Venus retrograde in your natal chart, this may be a signal that you will need space and time to process past relationship themes in this lifetime. You may need to put more effort and intention into relationships, because a retrograde planet means that the energy needs to mature inside of you so you can learn more and proceed with higher consciousness.

Retrograde Venus also means that, at a soul level, you have the opportunity to transform or adjust certain relationship patterns and themes. This can be very healing. You may be balancing karma, reviewing and learning from experiences that were left unfinished in previous lifetimes.

Venus Conjunct

Conjunctions occur when two or more planets appear to be traveling together from our perspective on Earth. A conjunction combines and amplifies the separate energies of the celestial bodies involved. If your natal Venus is in conjunction with another planet—especially another personal planet (Sun, Moon, Mercury, or Mars)—then Venus brings her loving energy to partner with that planet's intentions. Venus wants to soften and support any conjunct natal planets in some capacity. The quality of this interaction depends on the astrological sign the planets are in, but Venus energy always brings kindness, a soft touch, a sense of relatability, and beauty to that natal planet. Venus conjunct any of the personal planets is bringing in lessons of self-worth, self-value, and self-love.

In turn, other natal planets also support Venus when in conjunction. If you have Venus conjunct Mercury, for example, Mercury is going to bring words, thoughts, and ideas to the Venus quest for self-love and relationships. A Venus conjunction can also reveal the energies you want to experience, receive, and attract in a partner, since Venus rules relationships and connection. Venus conjunct the Moon can be nurturing, feminine, emotional, intuitive, and open, which may be reflected in the type of relationship dynamics you naturally want to experience and that you unconsciously attract.

Venus conjunct Mars is a very interesting energy, because Mars rules the masculine while Venus rules the feminine. Depending on which astrological sign they're in, this pairing will tend to favor a stronger masculine or stronger feminine energy. Fire and Air signs bring out stronger masculine energy; Earth and Water signs support stronger feminine energy. These masculine and feminine energies working together can feel either neutral, ambiguous, or totally harmonious. When Venus is conjunct the Sun, the shared sign's energy expresses itself through the physical self and physical energy. This conjunction shines a high beam on your lifelong task of learning to love and accept yourself with confidence.

Examine for a moment your own relationship experiences and see if you can determine how Venus has been showing up in your life. What are the themes? What are you working on and improving? What do you know now that you didn't know when you were younger? How are you taking responsibility for yourself? The roots of Venus are always growing, digging deeper into the soil of self-love and acceptance. Venus' branches extend into the clear air of understanding and reach toward others for connection and mutual love. Integrating and balancing this energy takes a lifetime of ongoing work, with opportunities for growth emerging through our relationships with others and our ongoing relationship with ourselves.

Chapter 8

The Twelve Venus Signs

Venus can reveal your lifelong path of maturing in relationships—both your evolving relationship with yourself and your connection with others. When you truly love and accept who you are at a core level, you are developing and growing your self-worth and revealing what is possible in your life. Venus energies help you recognize yourself more, which in turn allows you to connect more authentically with others. Venus wants you to feel good about who you are in this lifetime.

You can take ownership of your relationship with yourself. You can soften and ease into loving who you are—your unique essence, your flaws, all of it. Understand that you are absolutely worthy of love. You don't have to earn it or cultivate it. You can simply uncover its source deep within and honor your value and your worth. The stronger and clearer this love and worth shines within you, the more it will infuse your energy field and touch the roots and branches of the people with whom you connect.

Venus in Aries (Fire, Cardinal, Masculine)

Independent, Self-motivated, Fierce, Maverick

Those with Venus in Aries are here to do things their own way. They are independent and pioneering and often want to be in charge and lead. In fact, they may enjoy their independence so much that they lose sight of their need for help and connection with others. They tend to be good at working on their own and may be very selective about the types of relationships they enter into or are compatible with.

Venus in any Fire sign is going to be fierce, which can be read as inspiring and motivated, but can veer into a penchant for conflict as well. Aries energy raises its consciousness by looking for the deeper meanings at play. What are you fighting for and why? What are you fighting in yourself or in other people? Once you see this and understand it, you can choose to soften that fiery energy. Venus in Aries learns from the opposing sign of Libra to cooperate, to talk things out, to be aware of other perspectives, and to find a shared objective point of view.

If your Venus is in Aries, you may find that, at times, you don't want to be in relationships at all. You want to do your own thing without relating to others. As you mature, you learn that you can work with others selectively without sacrificing your independence, your uniqueness, or your needs. In fact, by bringing these qualities forward, you inspire and draw more people to you.

Venus in Aries awakens your Divine Feminine energies by revealing where you can be strong and independent without damaging relationships or unconsciously fighting others. Your higher expressions of the Divine Feminine want to be made manifest through inspiration and motivation, following your own truth, and encouraging others to do the same for themselves. You are a natural warrior and a maverick who can motivate people to be their best selves and inspire them to take appropriate action in their lives.

If your natal Venus is in Aries, you need to stay mindful of your competitive streak and your ego. Understand what you are fighting for, as these are masculine energies that you may unconsciously enact when you want something. Your Venus energies help you to see how you can be soft and tender, even in the heat of the moment. They teach you that you can connect with people in a more genuine manner when you put down your sword and shield. You are strong enough to go it alone, but you will need people and quality connections as well. You are learning that it is okay to share and receive from others and this does not make you less independent or fierce. In fact, it expands your heart and shows you that there are good people in the world whom you can trust with your dreams and ambitions.

◆ *Venus in Aries awakens through*: strength without conflict, inspiring others, softening into trust, collaborating with others.

Venus in Taurus (Earth, Fixed, Feminine)

Sensual, Comfort-seeking, Self-confident, Capable

Venus in Taurus is a very strong placement. Venus is at her best in this feminine sign, happily enjoying the pleasures of the five senses. You feel good receiving and you are generally secure in yourself in this Earth sign. Venus in Taurus knows how to create comfort in this life, whether it's through reliable relationships, financial stability, a secure lifestyle, or all three. But this Venus can tip into materialism, which offers artificial comforts that don't really bring true pleasure.

Those with Venus in Taurus are learning that, as much as they enjoy being in their own private world, they can open up and build connections with people who are trustworthy. They learn from opposing Scorpio energies to connect from a more vulnerable place. If your Venus is in Taurus, you are looking for others who share your values and way of life. But your tendency to focus on what can be experienced through the five senses can limit your search for deeper connection. Seek out ways to go deeper into what you feel—deeper into what is happening beneath the surface—and know that it can be rewarding to share yourself with others. You don't need to stay only in your own energies. You have the capacity to share and open up. Through multiple types of relationships, both romantic and platonic, you can understand more of what you value and find meaningful.

Those with Venus in Taurus are awakening to more of their Divine Feminine energies by trusting others to understand them and know them more intimately. Relationships are a playground of experiences, and you can always feel safe and secure in your own skin no matter what others choose or say. Your awakening process involves opening up in close connections and revealing more of what you need. It is okay to ask for what you want and to trust that you are worthy of receiving it. You are strong and capable, but also gifted with the ability to enjoy the best of life with the right people who have similar values. As you allow others to see the real you, your heart will feel more open and trusting of these interactions. Soften and open up to those you trust. Your journey will feel even more satisfying as people get to know the real you.

◆ *Venus in Taurus awakens through*: going below the surface, enjoying life's pleasures, allowing others to know you, softening resistance to change.

Venus in Gemini (Air, Mutable, Masculine)
Cerebral, Focused, Expressive, Inquisitive

If your Venus is in Gemini, you are an intellectual with an alert and active mind. You want to read, write, talk things out, express yourself, and share your ideas freely. You can also tend to live in your head, giving you a narrow focus on whatever's right in front of you. You're most likely searching for endless stimuli and interesting stories, including the current trends on social media, the newest books, and the latest research.

Because you have a lot moving through your mind and a variety of interests, you form friendships with many kinds of people. But being caught up in your thoughts can prevent you from dropping down into your heart. You can benefit from getting out of your mind and checking in with your feelings. You will grow through experiences in the world that stretch your mind and activate your heart.

Those with Venus in Gemini are learning from their opposing Sagittarius energy that it's good to take a risk, to try something new, and to have adventures beyond their normal routine that show more of what can be experienced and felt. As you drop into your heart and listen to your body, your desire to move will come alive, and you will find that you can break away from reading on the couch or staring at a screen. You will grow in rewarding ways through sharing experiences with others in relationships.

You are awakening to more of your Divine Feminine energies by softening into your heart space and speaking your truth from there. You are a natural intellectual and a gifted communicator, so your higher expressions of feminine energies will embrace how it feels to share more of your emotions and vulnerabilities with those you trust. Your Divine Feminine self is expanding into more of what you need to feel heard, seen, and acknowledged. You are trusting that it is safe to share more of yourself. Take time to listen to your deeper needs and be willing to share these parts of yourself with people to whom you are close. Your Venus energies give you the gift of self-expression and the ability to acknowledge the value of intimate communications.

♦ *Venus in Gemini awakens through*: sharing your intimate truth, expanding your horizons, expressing your needs, consciously using your voice.

Venus in Cancer (Water, Cardinal, Feminine)
Affectionate, Sharing, Emotional, Caretaker

Venus in Cancer is soft, loving, and kind, with a big heart that feels a lot. Those with this placement are sensitive to the environment and often desire a beautiful home and a safe space that feels good to them. When they feel open, they want to know that they can honestly share their hearts with others. It's very important to them to have relationships that honor their emotional world and give them the ability to express themselves as they ride the waves.

If your Venus is in Cancer, you can be moody, shifting with the tides. You may feel different every day of the week. You're tuned in to the bigger energetic cycles of the world. When you feel safe to be yourself and feel safe in relationships, this energetic connection to the world can bring deep joy and powerful insight. Without safety, however, it can feel scary. Your need for security is so strong that you may even feel self-protective in relationships at times, retreating into your personal world so that you can have space to move through your feelings.

As a Venus in Cancer, you can be very connected to your own mother or mother figure, or have strong maternal instincts. You may look for ways in which you can mother yourself in this lifetime, like honoring your feelings and taking care of yourself when you are hurt or upset. You are learning about energetic and emotional boundaries as you take responsibility for what is yours, and you don't expect others to take care of you. You may experience a repeating theme in your relationships of looking for a mother or someone to provide a safe womb for you. And yet your real challenge is to create and maintain that safe place by establishing your own boundaries.

You are learning that you do not need to be everyone's caretaker. No one benefits when you try to take care of others while sacrificing yourself and feeling depleted or resentful. You need to hold on to your energetic container and watch how you show up in relationships with others. Don't overextend yourself or try to be a caretaker. You are learning through the opposing sign of Capricorn to detach and allow everyone to be responsible for themselves. Capricorn is teaching you to balance your emotional experience with the bigger picture. As you strengthen your boundaries, you will feel an increase in your self-respect and your relationships will feel more healthy and loving.

In this sign, you are awakening to the beauty of your Divine Feminine essence through your softness and vulnerabilities. You can create beautiful connections with others when you feel strong enough to share what you really feel. Trust that others want to know more about you, especially as you embrace your authentic self. Your Divine Feminine energies desire deep connections, and you are open to sharing your soul in ways that others may not always understand at first. Honor yourself as you open your heart, but also embrace your gift of getting to the heart of a matter. You light the way for friends and partners when you speak from the heart. Treasure your ability to know people at an intimate level, and others will treasure this expression of Divine Feminine energies in you.

- *Venus in Cancer awakens through*: balancing emotion with perspective, maintaining boundaries, inspiring others, remaining strong in your own needs.

Venus in Leo (Fire, Fixed, Masculine)

Artistic, Strong-willed, Fun-loving, Outgoing

Venus in Leo is confident, proud, and strong. You have a driving need to feel recognized in relationships. You want to be seen and to be viewed through the strength of who you are. You show up through your creativity, your artistic expression, and your leadership abilities. You need to feel validated and have strong willpower and a guiding gut-level instinct. Those with this natal Venus

look for relationships that are interesting, inspiring, and fun, but that also help them feel good about themselves and what they bring to the table. They are very much aware of love and the joys of dating, and they know how to flirt. Their passionate energy wants to be cherished and adored. When they don't feel valued, recognized, or cherished, they can choose to sulk or they can choose to do more for themselves. If this is your natal Venus, learn to cherish yourself more, to break free of what other people think of you, and to feel passionate about life even when you're out of the spotlight.

With Venus in Leo, you are learning how to step back from being the center of attention and to open up to more ways of experiencing love than simple adoration. You can connect with other people through the heart in so many ways. Let go of any single definition of what love is and open up to all the love in the world through all types of relationships. Don't forget self-love. You can fill your own tank without relying on how someone else views you.

You are awakening to Divine Feminine energies that allow you to soften and relax from the heart. Your strength can be very commanding and, when it is coupled with Divine Feminine expressions, you are able to bring more people into your heart in an authentic way. You are gifted with knowing who you are, and yet you do not have to put on a show or wear a mask to be seen, loved, or acknowledged. When you feel an inspiration to share and connect with others, your Divine Feminine energies can feel regal and kind. When you share with others and acknowledge who they are, this validates both you and them. Your Divine Feminine energies are at their best when you are connecting with self-respect and trusting people. The more you give and receive equally, the more you will feel balanced in your energy field. You are beautifully gifted with knowing exactly who you are, but you can also allow energetic space for others to shine brightly and feel loved in return.

◆ *Venus in Leo awakens through*: taking off the mask, opening to all forms of love, giving and receiving equally, softening into a deeper need.

Venus in Virgo (Earth, Mutable, Feminine)
Service-oriented, Supportive, Caring, Healing

Venus in Virgo wants to be helpful, to contribute, and to be of service. Venus is strongly connected to self-care and what the body needs. Virgo relates to the physical self, as well as the mind. So Venus in Virgo can be a very strong placement for tuning in to your physical healing needs and how your body, mind, and soul work together. This invites you to love all of yourself and to be aware of any critical or limiting self-love messages.

Sometimes Virgo energy can be hyperfocused on whether something is "good enough." Your love and relationship journey will thus navigate guilt, perfectionism, and the desire to improve. Manage these messages for yourself and take time to bask in higher consciousness messages. You are a beautiful person in motion, just as you are, and every day you are taking care of yourself. Focusing on routines and healthy daily habits will lift you up. Be clear about what matters to you and how it can be enriched by your routines. Connecting to a higher vibration of self-love in the spiritual realms will buoy you as you go about your day. You are learning to widen your gaze beyond what you did or did not do and to see yourself as a beautiful energy field in human form. Accept everything about yourself, flaws and all, and release the critical messages.

Venus in Virgo is supportive and makes for a wonderful friend. In your efforts to help others live a good life, you bring forward solutions and remedies for how to handle life's stresses. Others appreciate you, and you are often the go-to person when problems arise, because you have a genuine knack for figuring things out.

Consider stepping back when you are putting too much pressure on yourself. Your instincts to take care of others and support them in concrete ways can sideline your own needs. Take a moment to validate yourself and notice what you have accomplished—a great job on a project, success improving a difficult process, finding a new path forward, or perhaps bringing a lot to the table that was helpful and beneficial. Acknowledge yourself, even in small ways, and remain aware of how you are valuable.

With Venus in Virgo, you need to practice staying openhearted in relationships and learn to balance your powerful tendency to reside in your head. Drop into your heart and check in with what you are feeling. There may be more going on beneath the surface, and you will feel more fulfilled when you combine your heart and mind with compassion.

As a Venus in Virgo, you are awakening to your Divine Feminine expressions through conscious self-care, acceptance of your body, and applying compassion to yourself regularly. Your Divine Feminine energies are directly related to accepting yourself at all levels of your being and seeing how perfect you are in all ways.

- *Venus in Virgo awakens through*: knowing your worth, accepting yourself as you are right now, tapping into higher-octave self-love, letting yourself off the hook as needed.

Venus in Libra (Air, Cardinal, Masculine)
Sophisticated, Giving, Peacekeeper, Connector

Friendly sophisticated Venus is strong in Libra, one of her astrological home signs. Libra is a masculine sign, while Venus is a feminine energy, so there is a strong interplay between the feminine and the masculine with this placement. Those with Venus in Libra excel at conversation, connection, creating win-win situations, and finding solutions while experiencing healthy relationships in all areas of their lives. Venus guides their process of learning how to remain true to themselves and their own self-identity, without trying to keep the peace or giving up what they need. They can be so focused on others in their relationships, however, that they forget who they are or what they want.

As a Venus in Libra, you are learning how to ask for what you need. You can be very aware of what other people want and how to please them, but relationships are a two-way dynamic. You must learn to give while also allowing yourself to receive. When you master this balance, you feel worthy of being seen and acknowledged.

Your Venus in Libra needs to talk things out, so it's important to have friendships, relationships, and connections full of lively, profound conversations. If your relationships are one-sided or draining, you can become unconsciously codependent. It is okay to back away from anyone who does not contribute equally. You benefit from mutual relationships, which require you to be honest with yourself if you're expecting someone to show up or to do something that is not really in tune with who they are.

Your Divine Feminine energies are beautifully expressed when you are open, sharing, and receiving. As you soften into yourself and trust what you need, you may feel that part of your energy relaxes into more of what your heart truly desires. You are awakening to the power of receiving and knowing that you are inherently worthy of having others provide for you. You may tend to hold back on articulating what you need, yet your Divine Feminine is guided to blossom so you can enjoy the unexpected ways in which you can be on the receiving end of unlimited abundance and joy. You are gifted with finding equilibrium and peace within yourself, and others will sense those energies in you. You will draw the right people to you when you are feeling open and grounded in all of your energy.

◆ *Venus in Libra awakens through*: letting others provide, remembering to ask for what you want, balancing giving and receiving, maintaining your sense of self and personal needs.

Venus in Scorpio (Water, Fixed, Feminine)

Intense, Private, Vulnerable, Driven

Venus in Scorpio is a passionate, intuitive energy that taps into an emotional world beneath the surface. With this placement, you are learning to trust yourself through the experiences of relationships as you go deeper into your own needs and emotional patterns. You are drawn to a wide array of relationship styles and attracted to all kinds of people, so you will experience vast ups and downs along your healing and self-worth journey.

The intensity of Venus in Scorpio can be a lot for others to take in and understand, but you have the opportunity to know and understand yourself without validation from outside. You need, and you are learning to create, a safe place in which to share how you feel, whether that is with a therapist, a counselor, a healer, or a trusted friend. You need to have a way to work through your emotions, especially if you feel jealousy or envy, so you can determine how to rise above them as needed.

The Scorpio journey is first about going deep into the root of your feelings and experiences. You may even be working with an accumulation of energies across multiple lifetimes and healing in a very deep way. This takes a lot of intentional work, because Venus in Scorpio wants to connect with people. You want intimacy and deeper sharing, but you are always evaluating whom you can and can't trust. You are often processing very deep fears in relationships, and this can show up as manipulation, betrayal, lying, control, abuse, and simply not trusting others. Trust ultimately begins with trusting yourself—your intuition, your emotions, and your gut-level instincts. The paradox here is that you can only experience healthy and trusting relationships with others by learning to trust yourself. Part of your work is to use whatever comes up in relationships to enhance your own self-worth, your self-love, and your self-acceptance.

Venus in Scorpio is learning how to be grounded. It's not necessary to dive into the deep end all the time. When you find yourself overly invested in others or consumed in a passion or an experience, you may want to pull yourself back up toward the surface. Operating at that depth nonstop can be draining. Stay mindful of how you're sharing your energy and how you're connecting with others, and make sure you're doing things in a reciprocal, healthy manner.

Your Divine Feminine energies are awakening to the powerful messages in your intuition and how to trust what you feel in a firm, grounded manner. Soften into yourself with a sense of strength and trust in your abilities. Because you are so porous and so powerful, it is important that you regularly reclaim your energies, taking them back from other people. Learn to cleanse your energies to ensure that you are not holding or absorbing what is not yours. You are awakening to deeper healing powers that can transform your desires into powerful manifestations. You will elevate to higher Divine Feminine energies as you focus on how you are worthy of healthy, loving connections in all areas of your life. As you open into this energy field, you will feel safer and more supported by the Universe.

- *Venus in Scorpio awakens through*: reclaiming your energies, trusting your instincts, resurfacing from the emotional depths, stabilizing your sense of self-worth.

Venus in Sagittarius (Fire, Mutable, Masculine)

Restless, Adventurous, Inquiring, Opinionated

Venus in Sagittarius is knowledgeable, independent, and restless. You may love being on the move as you are always ready for the next adventure and do not want to be tied down or held back in any way. Sagittarius is about what you learn and experience, and how it forms your understanding of the world. Venus in Sagittarius tends to seek out many types of relationships, always learning and collecting wisdom from each one. This Venus wants to grow and expand from interactions with a diverse group of people. Encountering differing viewpoints, opinions, and ideologies energizes you, although you will tend to maintain firm opinions around what you believe is right or wrong, appropriate or unacceptable.

As a Venus in Sagittarius, you see relationships as a source of growth. You may have a variety of love affairs, connections, lovers, and relationships, each of which offers you something different. You are independent and motivated, so you are choosy about people. You often desire to connect with someone based on shared beliefs, a similar worldview, and a sense of adventure for life. As you shift and change through life, your friendships and relationships will continue to evolve. Sagittarius energy needs to have space to roam and keep moving, so the best relationships for you will allow for and honor your independence. Nonetheless, a part of you desires true connection and long-term friendships.

Venus in Sagittarius is learning to talk things through, to listen, and to understand the specifics of other people's lives. When you can accept people as they are, you bring openhearted and expansive energy to your relationships. Do you tell people what they should and shouldn't do? Be aware of your unconscious expectations overwhelming people. You may be more comfortable than others are with broad expressions and bold opinions.

Your Divine Feminine energies are awakening to the myriad ways you can truly honor, love, and accept yourself and others. Connect with the beauty in each person as a unique light in the cosmos. This opens you up to all of your own potentials in this lifetime. As a Venus in Sagittarius, you may continue growing and learning, blossoming with age and more wisdom in a way that grants you a deeper acceptance of others. As your heart grows bigger and fuller, release attachments to and expectations of what someone else should be. Your Divine Feminine energies can soften into feeling supported by others on your journey and by not expecting yourself to do everything on your own. As you open up to deeper levels of trust, you will find that true friendships and authentic people will show up to connect with you, often for the long haul.

- *Venus in Sagittarius awakens through*: releasing expectations, opening into acceptance, exploring the varied details of others' lives, trusting your own personal journey.

Venus in Capricorn (Earth, Cardinal, Feminine)

Mature, Discerning, Reliable, Reserved

Venus in Capricorn tends to be mature, responsible, and serious, with a personal sense of integrity and self-respect. If this is your placement, you may feel like an old soul, as you often evaluate others or potential relationships thoroughly before moving ahead with a commitment. You may even be the maturer person in a relationship, regardless of your age—you may tend to take on more responsibility or be in charge of more energy. You are discerning and reserved, and may prefer to be alone rather than connect with someone you deem unworthy. But once you enjoy and feel comfortable with someone, you invest in the connection and make it a priority.

You may feel that you have a mature heart and that you want to be respected in genuine ways. It may take a lot for you to open up to others, especially as you focus on what you are achieving and working toward in life that is satisfying to you. In fact, you sometimes choose to be overly focused on your career in order to avoid relationships or intimate connections. You are learning how to be yourself in the world and with others, and you do not have to choose one or the other. You may only need a few select individuals in your personal circle. Capricorn energy is in it for the long term, so when you really connect with someone, you will stick with that person for a long time. You prefer reliability and stability in your relationships, and you expect others to show up with those same values.

Venus in Capricorn is learning to share and open up, so you may be drawn to people who encourage you to go deeper and not hold back what you need. You are learning that others can support you if you let them, and that asking for what you need is not a sign of weakness or incompetence.

As a sophisticated Venus in Capricorn, you can be very aware of how you come across and what others perceive. You are a careful observer of people's behavior. You don't want to play games, which translates into a maturity around how you interact with people in all areas of your life. As you age, you may grow comfortable and easy with your physical appearance, so you may be considered a classic beauty or very handsome. Energetically, you embody the wisdom of your experiences and the wisdom you have acquired through all types of relationships.

You are awakening to your Divine Feminine energies of feeling recognized, acknowledged, and supported in all areas of your life. As you soften into the wisdom that comes with time and experience, you may have shifting priorities around how you want others to know you and see you. You may let down your guard over something, or you may open up your heart more willingly. You are being guided to let people into your world and your heart, and to express your needs more openly, especially because you do not have to do everything on your own. Others want to support you in more personal ways. Your Divine Feminine energies are blossoming as you trust the soft places in your being and give trustworthy individuals access to more of your true self.

- ◆ *Venus in Capricorn awakens through*: letting down your guard, allowing others in, accepting personal support, softening into your heart for strength.

Venus in Aquarius (Air, Fixed, Masculine)
Dynamic, Trendsetting, Rebellious, Affable

If your Venus is in Aquarius, you are creative, dynamic, and independent to such a degree that you may be ahead of your time in some way. With your own sense of fashion, your beauty, your unique look, and your creative expression, you tend to stand out from the crowd. You are tuned in to what is coming up or what people will want next. You can set trends. You are probably not afraid of being different or expressing yourself through your physical appearance and style choices, and these qualities draw relationships to you.

Those with Venus in Aquarius can be everybody's friend, as their natural affability may connect them with a lot of people, a big network, or a broad social circle. They enjoy connecting in easy ways, but they may not want to have deeper connections with people who inhibit their independence or intrude on their personal lives. They need the space to do things their own way and the freedom to change plans. They want the ability to be unpredictable and a little bit rebellious, and they go off the beaten path when inspiration strikes. If this is your placement, chances are that your focus on the bigger picture of your life connects you with others through shared passions, ideologies, and fun adventures. You can be very inspired and driven, but you're also learning how to put all of your chatter and ideas into action without feeling that you're being pulled in multiple directions.

You are also learning to go into your heart and prioritize what you feel at times. Because so much is always running through your mind and your nervous system, it is wise to check in with your heart and listen for the answers within. If you talk and share regularly with your friends, make time to sit quietly and hear your own inner messages. You are learning to come into your heart and tap into your unique spark.

As a Venus in Aquarius, you are awakening to the Divine Feminine energies that reside in your personal needs and beginning to share what you want with others. You are learning to soften into your heart's messages and to communicate from a place of openness in a way that may make you feel vulnerable at first. Though you easily understand situations, relationships, and experiences because of your quick mind, your Divine Feminine growth is guiding you more into what truly lights you up in your heart and soul. Trust these messages in yourself, even when you can't articulate them in your mind. Your energy will continue to grow and flourish as you learn to trust what you feel, allowing your internal messages to direct you into more fulfilling relationships with others.

♦ *Venus in Aquarius awakens through*: tapping into your inner spark, prioritizing your desires, claiming your freedom, valuing your contributions and perspectives.

Venus in Pisces (Water, Mutable, Feminine)
Compassionate, Private, Supportive, Self-effacing

Venus in Pisces is kind, loving, and compassionate and willing to support others as needed. In this placement, you are intuitive, creative, and a great listener who can easily pick up on what others are feeling without it being spoken. Your ability to feel deeply allows you to connect with people and understand

more of who they are at a soul level. You can be sensitive, highly empathic, and aware of others. These qualities make you an amazing friend. At the same time, you will only be able to fulfill your own needs when you remain aware of what you're bringing into the relationship and allow others to give back to you. Your gift of intense feeling can be managed and balanced by integrating some detachment and discernment.

Venus in Pisces likes privacy, which may lead you to retreat from relationships if you're not getting your own space every day. Going off into your own fantasyland or something that takes you out of your daily reality can be rejuvenating for you, as long as it doesn't tip over into unhealthy or addictive escapism.

As a Venus in Pisces, you are learning how to honor your emotional world and to trust your feelings, while also having the strength to show up and share who you are completely. You are learning the importance of boundaries in relationships. You need to really look at who respects you and values you in order to ward off codependent or freeloading relationships. Practice discernment and observe behavior, and be honest with yourself when you are giving too much in order to keep a relationship afloat.

In this placement, you also run the risk of falling into idealizing others. Get curious about what people say, do, and choose. This will help ground you in the truth of who they are and is a powerful way to build trust in yourself. Part of your journey is understanding that you feel a lot of things. But you need to balance that with the energies of Virgo, which lies opposite Pisces on the zodiac wheel. Learn to accept people at face value and see things for what they are. Don't assume people are more than they are, and don't assume that they are beautiful and perfect just because you want them to be.

You are awakening to your Divine Feminine energies that support strengthening into your needs and your sense of self. You are loving and kind to others, but it is essential to give that compassionate energy to yourself as well. You are guided to own your power by knowing yourself more and accepting that others want to give to you. Receiving is essential to feeling worthy. Your Divine Feminine energies will continue to blossom as you see how powerful you are in every area of life. You do not need to hold yourself back or deny what you want in relationships or friendships. Listen to your own messages, and then be willing to let others hear you without downplaying who you are.

◆ *Venus in Pisces awakens through*: loving yourself, claiming your power in relationships, learning to detach and discern, developing strong boundaries out of self-respect.

PART FIVE

Your Mars Sign

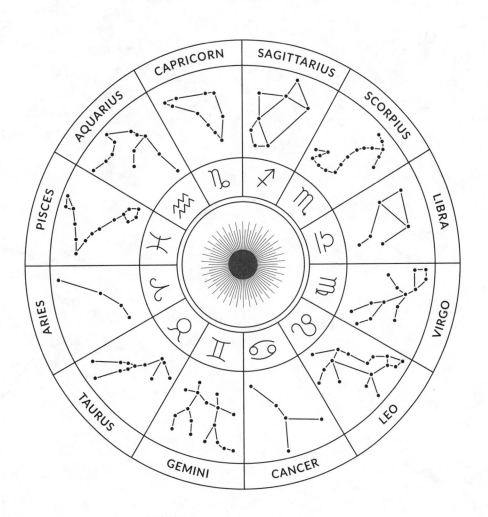

Chapter 9

Masculine Energies

Your Mars sign expresses masculine energies and determines how you navigate through life. Are you a low, speedy sports car, always in competition with yourself and others? Are you an ocean liner, heavily loaded and unphased by unpleasant weather? Or a light and airy bicycle maneuvering down a crowded city street, zipping between slower cars and trucks? Or perhaps you're a space-bound vehicle blasting off to explore and report back on your findings.

Imagine trying to explore the bottom of the ocean in a pickup truck. When you aren't aware of how your Mars energy is being expressed, you may feel frustrated and wonder why your approach to problems and your attempts to solve them are not successful. As you grow to understand the role of Mars in your chart, however, you gain a new persepctive on how you go about getting what you want and how your particular Mars energy moves through the world and works for you rather than against you.

Mars determines how you assert yourself and how you go after what you want in life. As an expression of masculine energy, Mars relates to desires, to the physical body, and to how you come across to others through the ego—either through a healthy ego or a false one fed by fear and insecurity. Mars can help you tap into your most productive states and make you more efficient. When you are in tune with your Mars energy, you can accomplish more.

Mars Retrograde

If you were born with Mars retrograde, your natural tendency is to turn inward first and consider the actions you are going to take before you move forward. Whenever a personal planet is retrograde, it typically indicates that you approach decisions and actions as a multistep process rather than a direct one. Those with a non-retrograde Mars assert themselves and plunge forward without thinking twice. Those with Mars retrograde choose rather to slow down, to be aware of how they apply their energy, and to be more conscious of how they express their masculine attributes.

Mars is associated with masculine expressions. And just as with Venus' feminine expressions, the placement and interaction of your Mars sign with the rest of your chart provides a more detailed picture of how these energies play out in your life. For instance, if your Mars is in a feminine astrological sign, this can provide a balance or neutrality between more receptive, internal feminine energies and more forceful, physical masculine energies.

Mars Conjunct

When Mars is conjunct one of the personal planets (Sun, Moon, Mercury, or Venus), it adds more dynamic momentum and self-assertion to that planet's energies. For example, if Mars is conjunct your Moon sign, chances are you need to be physically active every day—working out, being on the move, and even being more conscious of your emotional expressions. If Mars is energizing any of the personal planets, you may also need to be very aware of when it's time to slow down, when you're being too assertive, or when you're coming across as "too much."

By this time, you're getting a more layered picture of your personal astrological map. Your Sun sign is the container and guiding light of your life. Your Moon rules your emotional life and connects you to mother energies. Mercury determines how you communicate, while Venus shapes the way you connect in relationships with yourself and others. Your Mars sign guides you as you take action and put your ego forward in the best way. As you read about your natal Mars, keep in mind that there are healthy and conscious ways to express your masculine and feminine energies in alignment with the natural energy waves that are moving through you.

Chapter 10

The Twelve Mars Signs

How do you get things done? When you're in a tight spot, what qualities or hidden reserves kick in for you? What is your best strategy for attacking a problem? How does your healthy ego show up for you in relationship with yourself and others?

Your natal Mars attributes and how they relate to the rest of your chart address these questions. Mars will guide you forward with confidence based on your unique way of taking action. There are healthy, conscious ways to express yourself through Mars, especially as you become aware of what is truly working for you—and what is not. A well-developed Mars will lead you to better results, more trust in yourself, appropriate manners of self-expression, and an internal strength based on your ability to manifest what you deeply desire.

Mars in Aries (Fire, Cardinal, Masculine)

Impatient, Self-assured, Energetic, Impulsive

Mars is in his home sign in Aries. He's very comfortable here as the initiator, leader, and pioneer. Mars in Aries springs into action and wants to get moving forward, even to the point of impatience. If this is your natal Mars sign, you may act so quickly that you leave others behind in the dust. But even if you're comfortable zipping along in your own world, when it comes to interacting with others, you need to be aware of their pace and energy levels.

Since Mars represents the physical self, the body can be very strong when Mars is in Aries. Being physically active every day sustains the energy of this sign. In fact, if this energy is held back, it can bubble up in your emotional world as frustration, rage, and impatience. Throughout your life, you're going to need to learn how to temper the energy of your natal Mars. How can you rebalance yourself when you don't get your own way? How can you best manage anger? What are the healthiest ways for impulsive reactions to move through you? Moderating that quick-moving energy will pay off big for you. You'll want to use practices like meditation to bring you into your body, ground you, and relax you.

Mars in Aries energy can trust itself. If this is your natal Mars, you may use this energy to reach higher states of consciousness or to understand more about any first impulses you receive. Listen to your gut reactions and track how they flow through your body. You can build confidence in this intuitive mind-body connection through a physically challenging, artistic, or athletic pursuit.

Mars in Aries can be egoic and have a very strong sense of self. If you can stay mindful of how you may be coming across and temper self-involved thinking or actions, you are really going to feel inspired to follow what is correct for you and to trust yourself even more.

The Divine Masculine energies of those with Mars in Aries are best expressed through physical exertion, getting to know more about themselves, and embracing their leadership skills. They can lead others and can be powerful self-starters as they follow what motivates them to achieve. You may also feel adventurous, active, and ready to take a chance on something new. Divine Masculine energies are fortified through the Mars sense of self and the desire to feel strong in what you are capable of accomplishing. You also need space to do things your own way. Try not to be held back by others who operate at a different speed. Your energy excels at moving quickly, and you can be sure of yourself when you have the room to do things your way. Consider yourself a leader for others, even in an informal capacity, and embrace your courage and strength.

♦ *Mars in Aries awakens through*: moving your body regularly, tempering your anger or impatience, letting others catch up, allowing others to be heard and seen.

Mars in Taurus (Earth, Fixed, Feminine)

Persistent, Observant, Decisive, Determined

Mars in Taurus is a dedicated, focused builder. When you know what you want, there is no stopping you as you stick with tasks and priorities until they are complete. Mars in Taurus tends to be an observer, assessing the landscape before moving ahead with self-assured steps. You will move when it is essential and when you know the plan. You can be motivated to go after something you really want, especially something financial or material. Mars is invigorated by that which is held dear and can be very decisive. Taurus energy says: "No way, that's not for me" or "Yes, absolutely, I am determined to have it."

Mars in Taurus energies can also be stubborn, and even somewhat lethargic at times. If there isn't anything motivating your Taurus energy, you see no need to move from the couch just for the sake of doing so. But when something clicks and truly resonates, Mars in Taurus gets up, gets going, and sticks with it to the end.

Healthy Taurus energy connects to body awareness and maintenance. If this is your Mars sign, you may be motivated to work out, and you put in the time, energy, and effort it takes to care for your physical self. You may sometimes go after things for egoic gain, however—to appear a certain way to impress others or to load up on possessions that show off your financial status. As you mature, your values and priorities may shift toward healthier ego expression. When you get clear and dedicate yourself, your slow continuous efforts will pay off. At the end of the day, you can take enormous pride in the things into which you have poured your time, energy, and effort.

As a Mars in Taurus, your Divine Masculine energies are best expressed through your willpower, your reliability, and the self-love you express through physical actions. You are gifted with being a strong source of support, and you exude a calming manner that makes others feel safe. You can be the strong silent type, because you take in actions and information before deciding what to do next. This can give people a sense of trust in you. Continue to honor what calls to you, and allow yourself to move at your own speed. Your Divine Masculine expressions provide grounding and clarity in a world that is always changing and often chaotic. You are able to act with assurance and provide simple directions for a path forward.

◆ *Mars in Taurus awakens through*: moving at your own speed, supporting others, taking pride in valued accomplishments, knowing what is really worth your time and effort.

Mars in Gemini (Air, Mutable, Masculine)

Fast-moving, Multitalented, Impetuous, Shortsighted

Mars in Gemini is a fast-moving energy that is comfortable handling multiple priorities. Gemini is a multitasker, often doing two or more things at once, and then sometimes doing something twice in order to get the correct result. You can do one thing with your right hand and another with your left—metaphorically and sometimes even physically! Mars in Gemini feels comfortable navigating choices, seeing possibilities, and leaving options open. You do not want to be caged or held back, especially when you feel fired up to get something done. You may have an unconscious habit of starting a few things and moving on to the next idea before finishing what you started. You can sometimes move forward so fast that you forget why you started something in the first place. Gemini energy lives in the head, so Mars in Gemini needs to practice dropping down into the body and deciding where to put time and effort.

This Mars is good at getting things done quickly, like completing short projects or running quick errands. But Gemini energy can be flaky and forgetful and change its mind easily. So be sure your actions follow your verbal commitments.

A healthy expression of your Mars in Gemini shows genuine interest in what you're doing, loves being mentally stimulated by the task at hand, and grounds your busy mind in body consciousness. You can embrace a powerful dynamic between the mental and the physical as you learn to listen to your body. Body-scan meditations or other body-awareness practices help ensure an ongoing dialogue between your body and your mind, which reconnects you to your inner impulses and deep values.

Those with this fast-paced energy can benefit from putting on the brakes and looking down to make sure they're not tripping over their own feet. They sometimes need to double-check to make sure they're not missing anything. Keep an eye on the bigger picture so that you don't miss a chance to go farther or step out of your comfort zone and into a new, gratifying experience. Make sure that you're not moving so fast that you miss what really matters.

As a Mars in Gemini, your Divine Masculine energies can be expressed in a healthy way as you act with clarity and take care of commitments. You can gain productive momentum and build trust with others when you follow through on what you said you'd do. Avoid the temptation to say what others want to hear;

show them what you are capable of through your accomplishments. You can handle a lot at once, which is a strength, especially when you communicate your intentions to others. Combine your physical energy and strong mind with the ability to share what you are working on and why it is important. These qualities will be valued and respected and will invigorate you to accomplish even more.

♦ *Mars in Gemini awakens through*: following up on plans and ideas, keeping an eye on the bigger picture, connecting your mind and body consciously, remaining mindful of the commitments you make.

Mars in Cancer (Water, Cardinal, Feminine)

Receptive, Changeable, Cautious, Self-protective

Those with Mars in Cancer have an emotionally fueled energy that guides them to remain open to what feels right for them. Though they may not be quite conscious of it, they can put out their Spidey senses to determine what they're going to do next. Does it feel right? Is it safe? Is this something I want? You feel better when you have a sense of certainty before moving forward, and you may be comfortable waiting on the sidelines before taking action. Mars in the feminine sign of Cancer can be more receptive than assertive. If it feels right to you, you will go for it and see what happens next—although you may prefer to weigh potential outcomes first.

If your natal Mars is in Cancer, you are connected to the lunar cycle and its corresponding shifting daily energies. As a result, one day you may feel as if you're ready to jump into action and the next day you may feel that you can't possibly do anything—your energy just feels "off." Trust your body's messages and allow them to guide you. You don't need to adhere to other people's ways of moving through the world. Indulge your desire to move at your own pace, and set aside any routines that others want to force upon you. You prefer to navigate life based on what feels right and ride the waves as they appear.

Mars in Cancer needs to move emotional energy on a daily basis. This is important when you are feeling moody or excited or when a rising tide of energies sweeps through you. You're meant to process energy through your physical body so it doesn't get stuck, blocked, or backed up. Naming and releasing emotions as you dance, swim, jog, or do yoga can heal and empower you.

As a Mars in Cancer, you are learning to manage your reactions to the world around you as you mature. You may feel triggered, defensive, or vulnerable without always understanding why at first. Mars in Cancer energy wants to feel safe. You may avoid going after something directly, and instead skirt around the edges or come at it sideways, making sure everything's okay before acting. You don't want to be rejected and you're looking for what feels right. This internal dance can help you trust your body's messages.

Your Divine Masculine energies are learning to express themselves through honoring your feelings and acting from the heart. Your intentions are key. Share what you're experiencing and why you are going after something. Make sure other people know your intentions. Let people into your world so they can understand what matters to you. You may be self-protective, but you will build trust with others as you communicate your priorities and needs. Then you may feel even stronger in expressing your Divine Masculine strength and confidence and the power of authentic connections.

◆ *Mars in Cancer awakens through*: communicating what you need, coming at things more directly, trusting your body's emotional flow, remaining clear in your boundaries.

Mars in Leo (Fire, Fixed, Masculine)

Active, Assertive, Direct, Proud

Mars in Leo is very strong, as this energy tends to be active, motivated, and inspired. Leo has leadership energy, so Mars in Leo wants to feel in control and is comfortable taking the lead on priorities and tasks. If this is your natal Mars, you are assertive and direct. You go after what you want simply because it's what you want. You can really lead the pack down a path that excites you, so trust that in yourself. When something lights you up, follow the flow of energy. You may be drawn to anything that allows your light to shine, as well as to opportunities to command and direct.

That being said, you will always benefit from being aware of your effect on other people. Keeping your ego in check is key, as is noticing when you are operating from a false ego and when you're expressing your healthy ego. Bulldozing over people through your own power of will doesn't work well in the long run. There are ways to balance your determination and drive with the needs of others. Ease any opposition against you by keeping you ears open and your plans flexible.

Those with Mars in Leo need to be connected to their core values. Does this really have meaning to me? Do I really love this? Am I doing this for attention? Am I wearing a mask or performing a certain role in order to receive love? A healthy Mars in Leo will stick with the fixed energy of Leo to see things through to conclusion. The fixed signs lock in energy and use it to push through to completion. You can push yourself to the point of exhaustion, however, so you need to pace yourself. Be careful not to overdo, and put your time, energy, and effort into something that's in your heart.

Your Divine Masculine energies are strong, confident, and domineering. You can exude powerful leadership and are more likely to be admired when you are inclusive and consider what people need. The more you operate out of inspired actions rather than limited self-interest, the more others will trust you and gravitate toward your way of doing things. You can be very accomplished, because you have a clear idea of what you want and how to go about getting it. Physical exertion and releasing any pent-up energies will be an ongoing life priority for you. Your Divine Masculine expression can inspire and motivate others to try something new. You may naturally rise to the top in any area of life as you trust in yourself and allow room for others to be themselves as well.

♦ *Mars in Leo awakens through*: inspiring others to move ahead, taking off the mask, keeping your ego in check, acting from the heart and for the good of all.

Mars in Virgo (Earth, Mutable, Feminine)
Self-healing, Organized, Strategic, Thoughtful

Mars in Virgo can be a very healthy placement for anything you want to improve in your life, including your body, your healing abilities, your daily needs, and your overall self-care. Mars in Virgo strives to be healthier, stronger, and more organized. This can be a powerful energy for listening to what your body needs and making correct decisions for your health, well-being, and grooming. Mars in Virgo is very much about the details of the body, including how it works and how to heal it, but also understanding what really matters at the end of the day. You draw enormous strength from your daily routines and how you use your energy consistently.

Those with Mars in Virgo seek to organize, manage, and optimize the things to which they commit. They prefer to take the time to think something through and determine an efficient plan of action before they start. If this is your Mars sign, your strategizing mind paves the way in all areas of your life, and your physical energy follows in service of your highest priorities. You want to minimize missteps and not waste energy, so you often benefit from planning before proceeding.

It is also important to monitor how you handle stress, worry, and guilt. When you don't feel good enough, you may try to compensate by doing more or even by being more critical. Then your body can unconsciously harbor and hold these energies. You want to develop a healthy relationship with your physical self to ensure that you are not only hearing your body's messages, but developing daily habits to release the tension you tend to build up.

As a Mars in Virgo, your Divine Masculine energies can express themselves most clearly when you feel strong and grounded in your physical self. Taking care of your health is often a priority for you, and you can share your knowledge about healing and maintaining health with others. Mars in Virgo is gifted with demonstrating how consistent effort leads to ongoing rewards. You will feel a heightened level of personal integrity and self-respect when you follow through on your commitments and demonstrate your expertise. You can exemplify self-care and wellness abilities that ignite curiosity in others who want to imitate your practices and achieve the same results.

- ◆ *Mars in Virgo awakens through*: modeling healthy habits, releasing tension and guilt, taking action with compassion, responsibly helping and guiding others.

Mars in Libra (Air, Cardinal, Masculine)
Intentional, Social, Deliberate, Cocreative

Mars in Libra is graceful, intentional, and balanced. This is an interesting combination of energies because Mars wants to move forward, while Libra wants to sit and talk. So if this is your Mars sign, you may need to talk things through before you know which action you want to take. You may also gravitate toward partnered experiences or things you can do with other people. These connecting energies satisfy Libra's social aspect. Cocreating in multiple areas of your life, especially if you are comfortable collaborating, can increase your motivation and follow-through.

As a Mars in Libra, you may need to give yourself time to sit with a decision before you move ahead, and this can be beneficial for complex issues that need to be negotiated or planned carefully. You are deliberate and thoughtful and avoid running over others. You can be very considerate, listening and being aware of what needs to happen in a situation and then mapping out an appropriate plan. Learn to draw on the strength of Libra's Air qualities—your mental powers and gifts of communication. Incorporate these into your overall strategy for decision-making and taking action. An inability to make a decision can leave Mars paralyzed in Libra. You may shut down because of not wanting to upset somebody or create chaos. Remember that you aren't responsible for others, and that you can still move forward and trust yourself.

The Divine Masculine energies of this Mars are expressed in healthy ways as you seek favorable outcomes outside of conflict. You want to move ahead peacefully and seek the resources and inclination to make this happen. You can see things objectively before you go after what you want, which can help develop trust and respect with others. You come across as thoughtful and highly intentional. Your Divine Masculine energies can provide a sense of care and objectivity about what needs to happen next and how to go about it in a kind manner. Your Mars in Libra energies are gifted with being aware of other people's needs and knowing how to find creative win-win situations.

- *Mars in Libra awakens through*: collaborating with others, embracing objectivity, brokering peaceful solutions, taking clear decisive action as needed.

Mars in Scorpio (Water, Fixed, Feminine)
Driven, Productive, Committed, Capable

This natal Mars is very passionate, driven, and determined. Mars is strong in Scorpio, and you may have a one-track mind when it comes to going after what you want. Scorpio is intense, emotional, and operates with conviction. So you tend to have strong preferences, some of which may become obsessions. But Mars can be very productive in Scorpio, as well as strategic and intellectual. Your gift for observing other people's behaviors, choices, and feelings can aid your cause, or it can frustrate you. You latch on to external motivations like better finances, a new job, or a singular passion. Remembering your intentions and internal motivations will help make sure that you're not wasting your energy on something peripheral to your true goal—feeling powerful in who you are and what you want.

Because Scorpio is a fixed sign, you will stay the course and see things through; you do not give up or let go easily. However, there comes a time in every journey when letting one thing go allows you to move on to the next step. Similarly, you may have a hard time releasing what you have outgrown, especially if you do not know what you want next.

If this is your natal Mars, you will benefit from allowing any given process to unfold. Check in with yourself. Check in with what is really moving through you, and consider what you're ready to create next. Trusting yourself is key. When you do, you'll feel the surge of energy in your body that pushes you to move. Be aware, however, that you can be seduced into acting out scenarios of power, control, and manipulation. You may be drawn to go behind the scenes, to keep things hidden, or to be clandestine. You may rely on these tactics more than you need to.

The Divine Masculine energies of this placement flow best through healthy intentions that demonstrate your purpose and current passion. You can hold and exude a lot of energy, and people will feel how strong and capable you are. Your Mars in Scorpio can discern what is worth your time, energy, and effort and help you be very aware of why you're doing what you're doing. As you demonstrate your power and passion through successful achievements, you will also be operating with trust in yourself and your body. Use your Divine Masculine energy for the benefit of others, and you will experience even greater rewards and recognition.

♦ *Mars in Scorpio awakens through*: using your talents for others, allowing things to unfold with trust, learning to let go, passionately following what calls to you.

Mars in Sagittarius (Fire, Mutable, Masculine)
Explorer, Self-directed, Enthusiastic, Inspiring

Mars in Sagittarius is an inspired adventurer who does not want to be held down or held back. If this is your natal Mars, you desire the freedom to roam in whatever capacity suits you. You are often motivated to go beyond what is already known and peek over the neighbor's fence to discover something new and interesting. You go for what you want. Let's have an experience! Let's go on this trip! Let's move!

Mars is about going after what you want and Sagittarius has big dreams, so this combination can lead to a sense that there are big things in store for you in this life. You want to make things happen. You want to go for it, sometimes so much so that you overlook the details and practical steps that will get you there. In order to chase the dream, however, you have to take it step-by-step. Learn to step back and pay attention to what it will take to go on that trip, write that novel, build that company, or do anything else that reflects what matters to you.

In this sign, your body may naturally be drawn to movement, especially the legs and hips, which Sagittarius rules. So anything that opens up those energy streams and gets you moving will feel invigorating—going for a long walk, training for a marathon, good stretching exercises, or any type of dancing that may appeal to you.

Mars in Sagittarius may be up for anything, but this can dissolve into a kind of scattered energy that wants to do everything yet never accomplishes anything. When you feel yourself going in multiple directions at once, find a focus that reflects your values and your beliefs. When you understand those qualities in yourself, you're going to make sure that you are putting your time, energy, and effort toward a meaningful life. You may be motivated to learn something new, to gather knowledge, or to spend time in the natural world.

As a Mars in Sagittarius, you need to be aware of your ego, something that is true for Mars in all of the Fire signs. Think of a roaring fire that flares up and burns people. Bring awareness to any unconscious tendency to be pompous or righteous, or to hold on to illusions of grandeur. Balance your urge to share everything you've seen and done with healthy curiosity about the lives of others.

Your Divine Masculine energies are expressed in your confidence, your bravery, and your capacity to inspire others to live their best lives. You may motivate people to explore new areas of growth as they pick up on your enthusiasm for learning. Your energy is strong when you get people out of their heads and take them into new adventures and experiences. You are gifted with self-discovery and a growing confidence in yourself as you take risks in the world. Others will look to you for inspiration and guidance. Invite them into your world and open them up to even more within themselves along the way.

◆ *Mars in Sagittarius awakens through*: taking risks with trust in yourself, bringing others along for the ride, going step-by-step, managing multiple priorities with thoughtfulness.

Mars in Capricorn (Earth, Cardinal, Feminine)
Commanding, Trustworthy, Decisive, Accountable

Mars in Capricorn is the commander, the CEO, the manager who enjoys taking charge. This strong leadership energy makes plans, executes strategies, and knows how to move forward. If this is your natal Mars, you know how best to apply yourself to your long-term goals and stick with them. You can work with multiple people and many moving parts and bring them together on the same page to accomplish a goal. But it is important to consider others in this process and make room for differing thoughts, opinions, and desires. You know how to take action in ways that work for you, but you need to have input from others, although you would rather move on your own terms and be the one who decides. You can learn to incorporate the plans and viewpoints of others while maintaining your strength and positivity.

As a Mars in Capricorn, others trust you to be in charge, whether that is in the household, in an elected position, or in your career. You come across as capable, strong, and direct. However, you can also be forced to learn things the hard way if you're too headstrong or uncompromising. As you get older, the Capricorn influence will bring you more maturity and experience about how the world really operates and what things really matter to you. You will get better at picking your battles and listening to your collaborators.

Mars in Capricorn relates to the physical structure of the body—particularly bones, spine, knees, and teeth. Take care of this life scaffolding through good nutrition. Pay attention to things like calcium, the right vitamins, weight lifting, and a good doctor and dentist. All of this is important for the body's energy to move through you and to feel strong.

Your Divine Masculine energies make you a leader and a driving force for productivity. You exude a sensibility that others find alluring, including your understanding of how the world works and what is necessary to accomplish goals. You can accomplish a lot in your life because you are built for the long term and can handle life's adversities and challenges. Your Divine Masculine energies will fortify you in practical ways and allow you to guide others to move ahead with purpose and clarity.

◆ *Mars in Capricorn awakens through*: thinking long term about results, knowing how the world works, considering input from others, responsibly planning and following through on objectives.

Mars in Aquarius (Air, Fixed, Masculine)
Visionary, Original, Self-aware, Rebellious

Mars in Aquarius is independent and visionary, with an active energy that seeks out unique ways of doing things. You know what you want in life and feel fixated on going for it in whatever way works for you. You love to march to your own drummer and relish being outside the status quo. You trust any new path that looks invigorating and exciting. Aquarius energy is juicy, forward-thinking, and wants to try new things. As you branch out into the world, you can be ahead of the crowd and on the edge of what is to come next.

With Mars in Aquarius, you may have a very clear idea of what matters to you, including the outcome you want. This is how I'm going to go about this. This is what I'm going to make happen in my world. You may feel inspired to pursue an ideal by an internal thought, or you may see something out in the world that inspires you to create change or discover a fresh approach to a problem. Of course, other people's thoughts and ideas are going to be different from your own. Staying open to conversations and what other people have to offer doesn't mean that you have to change your plans. But you may discover useful feedback and even better solutions.

Mars in Aquarius can be very social. You may feel energized by interacting and sharing ideas in a group or by gravitating to community experiences. Be careful, however, not to fall into groupthink. You will also want time to yourself and need to feel like an individual. Both of these modes can serve you well.

With this natal Mars, you love to see things through to completion and have ongoing energy to do what needs to be done. But you also need to know when to stop, when to let something go. You need to recognize when something's over and you don't need to put more energy toward it. You can sometimes be so set on what you're creating and experiencing that it may be harder to step away and release when it's time to do so.

Mars in Aquarius can be original and rebellious. Your urge to do something better, to improve a system, to look at what isn't working, and to do what you can to make it better can lead to both a rocky and a rewarding road. If you see something as unjust or wrong, you have no problem taking action against it.

The Divine Masculine energies of this Mars stand in the strength of knowing what you want and trusting what calls to you. You are not here to blend in with the crowd; you're here to embrace what is unique and to take bold risks. Your Mars in Aquarius expressions are designed to break away from the crowd. Stand tall in your authenticity and the spark of life that motivates you. Others will be inspired to do the same, drawn to your magnetic and charming confidence.

◆ *Mars in Aquarius awakens through*: embracing your differences and unique style, taking on a cause, alternating between group and solo time, allowing others to be heard and seen.

Mars in Pisces (Water, Mutable, Feminine)

Trusting, Intuitive, Introspective, Inspired

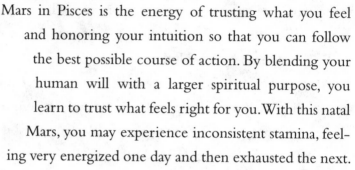

Mars in Pisces is the energy of trusting what you feel and honoring your intuition so that you can follow the best possible course of action. By blending your human will with a larger spiritual purpose, you learn to trust what feels right for you. With this natal Mars, you may experience inconsistent stamina, feeling very energized one day and then exhausted the next. Your motivation comes from a feeling or a bigger energy source that guides you forward, not from your head or logical thinking and planning. You know when to take action based on a feeling, a sense of timing, or even a synchronistic signal of support from the Universe that you can't miss. This is a very intuitively guided Mars.

Not everyone is able to trust their gut in the way that you can, however, so you may doubt your powers at times. As you mature, you'll learn to avoid the pitfalls of feeling powerless or falling into a victim mentality. You'll build your intuitive receptors so that, when that feeling comes through, it will motivate you, inspire you, and move you forward. When you trust your intuition deeply, you will find that things line up for you in staggering ways, because you're working with divine, not earthbound, timing.

This is often a very personal process. Is there a decision or action you took that seemed strange at the time, but when you look back on it, you see that you trusted yourself and did what was absolutely the correct thing for you? That's Mars in Pisces energy at work. That inspiration didn't come from overplanning or from anything in your head. You may encounter themes of surrendering throughout your life, times when you don't know how things are going to play out. But you feel what's right, and that feeling drives you forward to a successful outcome.

Mars in Pisces can suffer from low energy at times. There may be moments when all you can do is to sit on the couch and do nothing. Or you may need a lot of sleep. This is merely an indicaton that you're tapping into the influence of bigger energy cycles. Honor them. If there are some days you just can't do much, trust that, and know that it's part of your energetic makeup. You can be hard on yourself, but Mars in Pisces is telling you to trust your body and to respect when your body needs to rest. You may need more rest and more sleep than most people, and that's okay.

Just as with the other Water signs, Mars in Pisces makes you sensitive to your environment. Your spacial awareness may highlight strong desires or needs. Do you sometimes feel that you "can't be here right now?" Do you sometimes need to move away from a person or situation physically? Do you sometimes need to be in a space that is in alignment with who you are—one that is calmer, softer, or gentler? These all reflect the need of your Mars in Pisces energy to find and enjoy quiet space on a regular basis.

Those with Mars in Pisces move differently than others. The more you can trust this about yourself, the easier you can be on yourself. Free yourself from expectations of what something should be. Rather, make sure that you are in alignment with something higher—god, source, spirit, the Universe—and know that this energy is always going to lead you in the right direction at the right time.

Your Divine Masculine energies are amplified as you are guided to trust yourself on a very deep level in this lifetime. You are designed to take action on what you feel and sense is correct for you and to know that you have support along the way. This can be quite magical and amazing to observe, especially when you look back at how your life has lined up. Mars in Pisces moves through the world with a sense of mystical power, and it can bring you a wonderful ability to honor yourself. Trust your strength and partnership with higher consciousness as one of your gifts in this lifetime. Listen to how your body wants to move and feels energized as you go about your daily life. You are exuding what it means to move through life with a spiritual force.

♦ *Mars in Pisces awakens through*: trusting your intuition over your ego, slowing down as needed, honoring source energy, moving with your body's wisdom and needs.

Conclusion

The Awakening Continues

Astrology becomes endlessly fascinating the more you tap into the magic of your own energy. You gain new understandings of yourself by knowing more about your personal planets, especially as each one may begin to "speak" back to you. As you get to know more about the multiple layers of your energetic self, you start to hear more of your own wisdom and find that your needs express themselves in new ways. New conversations begin within.

For example, you may feel new insights from your Moon sign that beautifully translate the energy you are receiving while in conversation with a good friend. Your Venus may be gently guiding you toward greater inner harmony in all of your meaningful relationships as you get to the heart of what you need to feel truer connections. Mercury the Messenger may consciously connect you with a different viewpoint during a disagreement with a coworker, and you can tap into a new approach to resolve the discord. Mars may speak to you through inspired actions that you would not have considered before, yet that begin to feel more natural and effective. You may feel more confident and vibrant in the light of your bright Sun as you trust yourself even more and open up to the natural gifts you are here to express and share.

Your five personal planets together form a unique perspective that will continue to grow and change the more you awaken to yourself. Your Sun's soul growth points create a higher awareness in you and reveal ways for you to feel supported and powerful in your energy. Your Moon sign themes help you identify whatever may have been living in your unconscious that you can now bring into the light of that new self-awareness. Your Mercury awakens you to broader understandings and perspectives of which you may not have been aware, helping you to develop a sense of trust in what you do not yet know or see. Your natal Venus connects you to more of your Divine Feminine energies, enabling you to create more trust, confidence, and peace in your world and gain greater clarity and a deeper self-acceptance. Your natal Mars—a powerful force of action, desire, and vitality—shows you how to embody more Divine Masculine energies and achieve more self-respect, more integrity, and more self-confidence.

Astrology offers an ongoing adventure in consciousness, filled with unexpected twists and turns as you journey farther down this rabbit hole of ancient knowledge. Significant personal transformations are possible through this rich art—and they keep unfolding. Embracing each of your personal planets opens you up to more of your own energy as you consciously connect to more of the gifts, abilities, and attributes that support who you are in this lifetime. As the conversation continues, you will start to hear new messages and feel higher vibrations of what is possible for you. Just as the Sun, Moon, and stars keep shining and moving through the cosmos, you will find yourself connected to the larger cycles that support your ongoing soul growth and awakening in this lifetime.

Acknowledgments

"Look Mommy, it's a crescent moon tonight!"

Every time my son points up at the sky with these types of declarations, I feel so much gratitude that this sweet soul came into my world, and I get the honor of being his mom in this lifetime. I look forward to all of the adventures we have yet to cocreate together.

Because of my own experiences now as a mother, I can truly say how grateful I am to have a mom that has always been there for me as a guide, mentor, friend, and ally. Thank you for everything you have done through the decades, Mom, especially all of the ways you have supported the truth of who I am and truly "seen" me. I love you and Tom for being the fantastic people you are in the world.

Thank you to the beautiful souls in my life who are true friends and shining stars with genuinely good hearts. I am grateful to call you friends in the truest sense of the description, especially when we speak the language of astrology, energies, and spirituality together. Sending hugs to Sass, Rehana, Natali, Ava, Lori, Mari, Trisha, Sharon, Kathie, Brenda, and Madisyn.

The astrology community is an ongoing source of inspiration for me, especially since social media has allowed us to connect daily and navigate these wild energies together. Even though I am not able to thank each of you personally (or by your social media account names), I want to give a deep bow to those who connect and listen regularly through my weekly podcast episodes, YouTube videos, and online platforms. I appreciate you—and I never, never, never take it for granted that I can offer you something valuable for your own mastery. Onwards we go!

Finally, thank you to Randy Davila for your expertise and publishing guidance that started many moons ago, before I had the pleasure of connecting with you personally. And another round of gratitude to everyone on the Hierophant Publishing team who contributed to creating this book. Thank you for helping to make this final version even better than expected.

About the Author

Molly McCord, M.A., is a best-selling author of ten books, intuitive astrologer, modern consciousness teacher, and business guide who has hosted a successful podcast since 2012. She has studied and practiced astrology for over thirty years now, beginning with her first foray into the Sun signs in her early teens and continuing on by studying with mentors and other astrologers for decades. Molly lives in Florida with her young son who wants to know what your favorite dinosaur is today, and what your favorite dinosaur will be tomorrow. You can connect with her on Instagram, YouTube, Facebook, and her website at *www.MollyMcCord.online*.